WATERFALLS
of the BLUE RIDGE

A Guide to the
NATURAL WONDERS *of the*
BLUE RIDGE MOUNTAINS
5TH EDITION

JOHNNY MOLLOY

MENASHA RIDGE PRESS
Your Guide to the Outdoors Since 1982
an imprint of AdventureKEEN

Waterfalls of the Blue Ridge

Copyright © 2021 by Johnny Molloy
Copyright © 2014 by Johnny Molloy
Copyright © 2003, 1996, 1994 by Nicole Blouin
Printed in China
Published by Menasha Ridge Press
Distributed by Publishers Group West
Fifth edition, second printing 2023

Cover design and maps: Scott McGrew
Cover photos: © Johnny Molloy; *front:* Fenwick Mines Cascade (Trip 29, page 77);
  back: Chestnut Creek Falls (Trip 36, page 89)
Interior photos: © Johnny Molloy, unless otherwise noted on page
Text design: Annie Long
Project editor: Holly Cross
Copy editor: Kate Johnson
Proofreader: Emily Beaumont
Indexer: Rich Carlson

Name: Molloy, Johnny, 1961– author.
Title: Waterfalls of the Blue Ridge : a guide to the natural wonders of the Blue Ridge Mountains /
    Johnny Molloy.
Description: 5th edition. | Birmingham, AL : Menasha Ridge Press, 2021.
Identifiers: LCCN 2020052142 (print) | LCCN 2020052143 (ebook) |
    ISBN 9781634043298 (paperback) | ISBN 9781634043304 (ebook)
Subjects: LCSH: Hiking—Blue Ridge Parkway (N.C. and Va.)—Guidebooks. | Trails—Blue Ridge Parkway
    (N.C. and Va.)—Guidebooks. | Waterfalls—Virginia—Guidebooks. | Waterfalls—North Carolina—
    Guidebooks. | Blue Ridge Parkway (N.C. and Va.)—Guidebooks.
Classification: LCC GV199.42.B65 B56 2021 (print) | LCC GV199.42.B65 (ebook) | DDC 796.5109755—dc23
LC record available at https://lccn.loc.gov/2020052142
LC ebook record available at https://lccn.loc.gov/2020052143

🌳 **MENASHA RIDGE PRESS**
An imprint of AdventureKEEN
2204 First Ave. S., Ste. 102
Birmingham, AL 35233
800-678-7006, fax 877-374-9016

Visit menasharidge.com for a complete listing of our books and for ordering information. Contact us at
our website, at facebook.com/menasharidge, or at twitter.com/menasharidge with questions or com-
ments. To find out more about who we are and what we're doing, visit blog.menasharidge.com.

SAFETY NOTICE Although Menasha Ridge Press and the author have made every attempt to ensure
that the information in this book is accurate at press time, they are not responsible for any loss, dam-
age, injury, or inconvenience that may occur while using this book—you are responsible for your own
safety and health in the wilderness. Be aware that trail conditions can change from day to day. Always
check local conditions, know your own limitations, and consult a map and compass.

Table of Contents

List of Maps

Acknowledgments

Thanks to Menasha Ridge Press for the opportunity to add more than 20 waterfalls to this iconic tome that has led the way in waterfall guides for decades. I would like to express particular appreciation to the previous authors of this guide: Nicole Blouin and Marilou and Steve Bordonaro.

Thanks also to all the outdoors enthusiasts among us who hike the trails, take the photographs, and revel in being near one of God's great joys of nature—the waterfall.

—*Johnny Molloy*

FALLS OF WILSON CREEK *(see Trip 37, page 91)*

DRY FALLS IN WINTER *(see Trip 99, page 202)*   photo: Brenda J. Wiley

Preface

Waterfalls are perhaps nature's most captivating wonder. They are magical, holding all the secrets of the woods. Although they seem simple—falling water—we are astonished at finding these moving spectacles brightening the folds of the forest.

Mountain streams leave their birthplace, stretching and rushing toward the sea. They are fed by springs and rains as they travel down ancient slopes, following channels carved out centuries before. Reaching a precipice, they fall, creating an enchanting place.

For some people, waterfalls are simply excellent places to picnic. For others, they are the moving focus of all wild places. Whichever the case, waterfalls make you feel good. Their allure is similar to the cozy glow of a toasty fire, the endless rolling of the ocean surf, or a drumming rainstorm.

Add hiking and you double your pleasure. Most of the hikes in this book could stand alone, but they are even better when combined with the chance to visit a waterfall. Waterfall hiking in the mountains of the Blue Ridge is a marvelous way to experience the outdoors.

With this guide as your reference, you can seek out a different waterfall every time or hike to a favorite fall over and over, bringing friends and family. During an early morning walk, you might catch a glimpse of a wild animal drinking from a pool below the falls. Or you could camp beside a waterfall and fall asleep to the sound of rushing water.

Waterfalls often have interesting names, sometimes more mysterious than telling. Silver Run Falls has a beautiful name; Schoolhouse Falls has an unusual name; Big Rock Falls denotes a physical characteristic, while Bent Mountain Falls is named for a physical place. Like many waterfalls, Lower Cullasaja Falls and Soco Falls get their names from American Indian words. Others share common names, such as Upper Falls or Cascades. When setting off to see a waterfall, keep in mind that there may be another with the same name elsewhere and the falls may be known locally by a different name or simply as "the waterfall."

Each waterfall has its own personality. Some are exceptional for the water volume they command, others for the tremendous height from which they fall. The personality of a waterfall changes with each rainfall. Rain saturates the ground and feeds the creeks and rivers. Falls swell with an abundance of water: a delicate cascade might be a raging waterfall on the next visit, and vice versa. Thus, waterfalls invite visitors to return again and again.

The personality of a waterfall also changes with the seasons. The colors reflected in a clear mountain stream shift from pastels and greens to earth tones and shades of autumn. As the months progress, foliage around the falls blooms, flourishes, and withers away. One month, a flower grows out of a crack in the rock, watered by the constant spray of the falls; in another, an icicle hangs overhead.

Visit a waterfall in the spring and you'll see a pink-and-purple procession of flowering mountain laurels and rhododendrons. Waterfalls overflow from April rains, which bring May wildflowers to blanket the earth. The hillsides cry out for a wedding. In the summer, you'll enjoy the cool mist that drifts lazily off the face of the falls. This time of year, you can allow the waterfall to absorb you. Sink into the swimming hole at the base of the falls, lean back, and let the water cascade over you.

Visit a waterfall in autumn to be surrounded by the brilliant reds, yellows, and oranges of the hardwood forest. Color frames the white frothy cascade; painted leaves swirl and dance on the surface of the clear stream. Lie on a warm rock and bask in the sun for a while. The days of Indian summer, with crisp air and cloudless skies, beckon woodland adventurers. Subdued by winter, the wilderness offers wonderful solitude. Waterfalls freeze to create picturesque sculptures dangling from rocky cliffs. Snow blankets the forest floor, and bare trees provide unobstructed views.

The hills of the Blue Ridge harbor an incredible number of falls. Visitors, and even locals, are often unaware of how many extraordinary cascades adorn the area. The waterfall "collector," filling a personal list, will find heaven in the Blue Ridge, where hundreds of named waterfalls, and perhaps thousands more, are waiting to be discovered any time of year.

We've never met a waterfall—grand or gorgeous or graceful, bubbling brook or roaring river—we didn't like.

Introduction

Welcome to the fifth edition of this book, a collection of more than 140 waterfalls in the Blue Ridge Mountains. More than 20 were added for this new edition. The others were updated. New photos were added. The waterfalls range in height from 10 feet to 500 feet. Some require no hike at all, while others can only be seen from the trail, with hikes of up to 10 miles round-trip. For the purpose of this book, we roughly defined the Blue Ridge as the mountainous region along the Blue Ridge Parkway between Great Smoky Mountains National Park and Shenandoah National Park.

Waterfalls of the Blue Ridge will take you to two states, Virginia and North Carolina (plus a couple of waterfalls in South Carolina within walking distance of North Carolina); five national forests, George Washington, Jefferson, Pisgah, Nantahala, and Sumter; three national parks, Shenandoah, Blue Ridge Parkway, and Great Smoky Mountains; eleven state parks, Douthat, Grayson Highlands, Natural Bridge, New River Trail, Chimney Rock, Hanging Rock, Gorges, South Mountains, Stone Mountain, Mount Mitchell, and Caesars Head; four wilderness areas, Saint Mary's, Three Ridges, Linville Gorge, and Southern Nantahala; a state forest, DuPont; three Nature Conservancy tracts, Falls Ridge Preserve, Bottom Creek Gorge and Florence Nature Preserve, and the Cherokee Indian Reservation.

The waterfalls are grouped together according to their proximity to a particular town or their location in a state park or national park. Each chapter describes the waterfalls of the base town area with directions, including GPS coordinates. The waterfalls appear in geographic order, north to south.

To arrange a day of waterfall hiking, look under the chapter for the base town or park you plan to visit. Using the maps and information provided, you can plan hikes that fit your time limitations and physical ability. Choose a waterfall trail on which to spend the whole afternoon, or chart out a circuit and visit several in one day. We've provided trail distances and difficulty, waterfall descriptions, and directions to the trailheads.

TRAIL DISTANCE

The mileage listed for each hike is recorded as the total distance, round-trip (there and back along the same footpath or on a loop). To estimate how long it will take you to hike a certain distance, take into account your hiking style, your physical condition, and the trail conditions. The average hiker covers about 2 miles per hour, less with children or older hikers, and less carrying a fully loaded backpack when overnighting in the Blue Ridge.

TRAIL DIFFICULTY

The ratings for trail difficulty are based on the amount of energy expended by an average, healthy person. More effort is needed for each level: easy, moderate, and strenuous. Trail difficulty generally reflects elevation gained per mile. The longer and steeper the grade, the more difficult the trail is.

> **EASY** It is possible to hike an easy trail without getting tired. The gradient is generally flat with slight inclines.

> **MODERATE** You may be somewhat winded and need an occasional rest on a moderate hike. The trail will have some modest inclines.

> **STRENUOUS** The average hiker will definitely feel the workout on a strenuous trail. Several breaks may be necessary. The trail will have steep sections.

WATERFALL DESCRIPTIONS

Waterfalls are often described using a stack of superlatives: the highest, the widest, and the most beautiful. Such descriptions often neglect details and overlook the character of a waterfall. We tried to be informative by using specific details. Each waterfall description gives an estimated height of the falls and other details such as width, number of tiers, average flow, and angle of the falling water. Often we found a story behind the falls.

Most people prefer a waterfall with lots of volume, but the beauty of a waterfall is not necessarily tied to its rate of flow. Some waterfalls are always powerful, while others fluctuate dramatically with rainfall. If you want to see a waterfall at its most forceful, visit in the spring. Or watch the weather. Sometimes it just takes one good thunderstorm.

DIRECTIONS

This guide aims to get you to the waterfall or waterfall trailhead as easily as possible with clear, concise directions. These detailed driving directions, along with GPS trailhead coordinates at the end of each waterfall entry, will get you to the trailhead. The location of a trailhead is always indicated. Maps at the beginning of each chapter help you identify the falls relative to one another, as well as the surrounding towns and roads. However, the chapter maps are not intended to replace the driving directions. General trail information, positioned within the waterfall entry, will get you to the waterfall.

To find out more about a waterfall, a trail, or an area, go to the back of the book. Page 222 lists websites, addresses, and phone numbers for the parks mentioned throughout.

WILDERNESS ETHICS AND ETIQUETTE

More and more hikers visit the mountains of the Blue Ridge every year. Waterfall trails are especially popular destinations. The problems of overuse—soil erosion, overcrowding, litter, and decreasing numbers of wildlife and vegetation—are evident at some scenic spots. Wild places are for solitude and splendor. Those who love wild places can help preserve them.

In addition to the following list, we encourage you to consider doing two things. First, consider adopting one waterfall trail, officially or unofficially, that you can hike at least four times a year. Volunteer with the park headquarters, when applicable, to perform trail maintenance. And second, on your waterfall hikes, carry a trash bag and spend a few minutes picking up after someone less courteous. A little effort makes a tangible difference.

Stay on maintained trails. Safeguard against crushing sensitive plants and increasing soil erosion by not straying from designated paths. Trail builders strive to create a path that has good erosion control and as little impact on vegetation as possible. Do not walk off the trail, even to avoid muddy stretches, because this destroys the border and enlarges the trail. Switchbacks are the most often abused trail sections. Avoiding the temptation to take a shortcut can prevent future scars on the hillside.

Travel quietly in the woods. You are less likely to intrude upon other hikers, as well as the wildlife, when you walk and talk quietly. When taking a break, be courteous of those passing by. Don't block the trail or block someone's view of the falls with your picnic.

Hike during the off-season. Help spread out visitor use by taking advantage of the off-season. Off-season doesn't necessarily mean winter. Try going on weekdays, very early in the morning, or during rainy weather.

Travel in small groups. You lessen your impact on the trail and on other visitors when you are not hiking with a crowd. Large groups (10 people or more) cause a disproportionate invasion of narrow trails and small overlooks.

Pack everything out. You can contribute to the beauty of the woods by not adding anything. This principle includes biodegradable material; food scraps are unsightly and attract pests. Don't bury leftovers because animals may dig them up. Plan ahead: reduce the amount you pack in and carry a bag specifically for packing out waste.

Respect wildlife. When you enter the wilderness, you are traveling in other creatures' homes. Try to minimize your impact on wildlife. It is particularly important not to feed wild animals, for your safety and theirs.

Leave the things of nature in their place. You afford others the opportunity to enjoy the same experience that you enjoyed if you do not disturb the natural environment. If every hiker dug up a flower or collected an edible plant, we would quickly deplete an area. Take a photograph of the fire pink and only an occasional sample from the blackberry bush, and you will help protect the vegetation of our backcountry.

WARNINGS AND WATERFALL SAFETY

Oh, no! More rules? That's what we thought. But after talking with rangers, park employees, and city officials throughout the Blue Ridge, we discovered that accidents around waterfalls are a serious problem. Don't climb on slippery rocks or atop falls. Lovely waterfalls often hide lethal danger. Virginia's Crabtree Falls has claimed more than 30 lives since the U.S. Forest Service began keeping records in 1982.

Also remember that developed areas can be just as dangerous as undeveloped areas. As one ranger put it, "It is just the nature of rocks and water and cliffs. You can build observation decks and post signs, but people will be careless and use poor judgment."

The hazards are real, and we urge you to be careful. But instead of incorporating "a single slip could be your last" into every chapter, we decided to outline the basics of waterfall safety here.

- 💧 **STAY ON DEVELOPED TRAILS** and don't stray from observation points or platforms. Do not cross barriers—they are there for a reason.

- 💧 **WATCH YOUR FOOTING.** Rocks may be slippery, and algae-coated areas are unforgiving.

- 💧 **THE TOP OF ANY WATERFALL** is, of course, the most dangerous part. Avoid the temptation to lean over a ledge at the top of the falls.

- 💧 **EXERCISE CAUTION** on the trail to the falls, as well as around the falls themselves. Waterfall trails are often treacherous—steep and rocky with sheer embankments.

- 💧 **BE ESPECIALLY CAUTIOUS** when taking photographs. You are likely to pay more attention to your camera than to your footing.

- 💧 **WATCH CHILDREN CAREFULLY.** Children should always be under the immediate supervision of an adult.

- 💧 **WATCH YOUR DOG.** Our golden retriever, who was sure-footed but didn't understand the concept of slick rocks, fell off a 12-foot drop. He was fine, but we were nearly injured scurrying down to him.

- 💧 **NEVER HIKE ALONE.**

On any hike, carry a small day pack with useful items and extra gear. Most people consider these 10 items essential: lighter, compass, map, knife, flashlight, sunglasses, fire kindling, extra food, extra clothing, and a first aid kit. Add plastic baggies to the list for waterproofing and organizing. And be sure to carry an adequate supply of water. Don't drink any surface water unless it has been boiled for 1 minute or treated.

Do not count on a smartphone for your safety. Wireless reception may be spotty or nonexistent on the trail, even on a waterfall walk near a town or an interstate.

The preceding list may seem long, but the first six essentials can fit into a zip-top plastic bag. Extra food and clothing (a few candy bars and a raincoat or fleece) don't take up much space. Avid hikers sometimes keep a day pack filled and ready to go. Check the contents occasionally, testing batteries, restocking first aid supplies, and adding to food reserves as necessary.

PHOTOGRAPHING WATERFALLS

We photograph every waterfall we visit, preserving the collection on our computers and printing and framing our favorites. Not all photographs we take are great, just snapshots to preserve a memory. We've spent a lot of time shooting waterfalls, but getting an excellent shot takes time, effort, and luck.

For the best effect, you need a tripod, a digital camera with manual settings, and early-morning or late-afternoon light. Capturing the personality of a waterfall may mean several visits at different times of the year. The photographs in this book are the result of years of hard work, early-morning wake-up calls, and lots of shooting and reshooting.

HOOKER FALLS *(see Trip 83, page 171)*

In the process, we gained some solid insight that relates directly to water-fall photography. Here is a summary of the basics.

Tripod You'll need a sturdy tripod because your hands can't hold a camera sufficiently steady when using slow shutter speeds. Be sure the tripod is compact and lightweight so you'll be willing to carry it with you no matter how long the hike. Use a cable release, a cord attached to the shutter button that separates you from the camera. Better yet, set your camera and use a timer. This reduces shaking caused by pressing the shutter button. Our tripod rule: Use a tripod whenever you can, especially if the shutter speed is less than the lens focal length. For example, don't hand-hold a 50-millimeter lens when using a shutter speed slower than $\frac{1}{60}$ of a second.

ISO speed The ISO setting on most modern digital cameras is designed to approximate the ISO speed of a chosen film and corresponding camera setting used in a traditional film camera. The lowest ISO number you'll find on a digital camera, usually 100 but sometimes lower, is generally the preferred setting for shooting waterfalls. This number will yield the greatest detail, sharpness, effects, and color accuracy.

Shutter speed Slow shutter speeds give a sense of movement. Mike Wyatt, in his book *Basic Essentials of Photography Outdoors,* explains how shutter speed relates to moving current: "The movement of flowing water will be completely stopped at $\frac{1}{2000}$ second. The fastest portions of the water will begin to soften at $\frac{1}{60}$ second. At $\frac{1}{15}$ second, the water's movement will be clearly evident, but the water will not be completely blurred." Most waterfall photographs are shot at $\frac{1}{8}$ second or slower to produce a soft quality.

Time of day Midday sun creates harsh lighting and shadows. Visit a waterfall at daybreak or an hour before sunset, and observe the wonderful quality of the light. The light is softer, and colors are richer. Cloudy days afford more photo opportunities.

Exposure The white water of a falls will often cause underexposure of your shot, making the water gray and the foliage slightly dark. With digital cameras you can immediately see what you just shot and adjust aperture, shutter speed, or ISO setting.

Perspective Waterfall photographs need a reference to indicate their size. To give a feeling of depth and space, use foreground elements, such as trees, rocks, and people. In essence, try to frame the waterfall.

Position Shoot from the top, bottom, or side of the falls, but always try to keep one side of the image frame parallel to the ground. Basically, treat the waterfall like a piece of architecture. Be creative and see if you can shoot the fall from a different perspective.

People The high reflectance of water tends to underexpose people in a waterfall photograph. When positioning people, consider proper lighting for both your subjects and the waterfall.

Rainbows If you're lucky enough to find a rainbow at the end of a waterfall, take as many pictures as you can. Don't miss the opportunity for a spectacular photograph. Shoot at different settings and then delete pictures back at home.

Other notes Watch the sun, because light reflecting in the lens between the glass surfaces can cause a flare (diffused spot) or a ghost (multisided bright spot); look for the sun in the periphery. Watch the horizon; horizon lines should be level and, in general, not placed in the center of the composition. Middling skies have no place in a great photo; if the sky isn't deep blue, contrasted by white clouds, or intensely colorful, compose your shot without it. In the image area, look for wasted space, light and dark areas, and distracting elements. Before you take your photo, follow the rectangle of the viewing screen with your eyes.

Virginia Overview Map

See the Table of Contents and individual area maps for keys to numbering below.

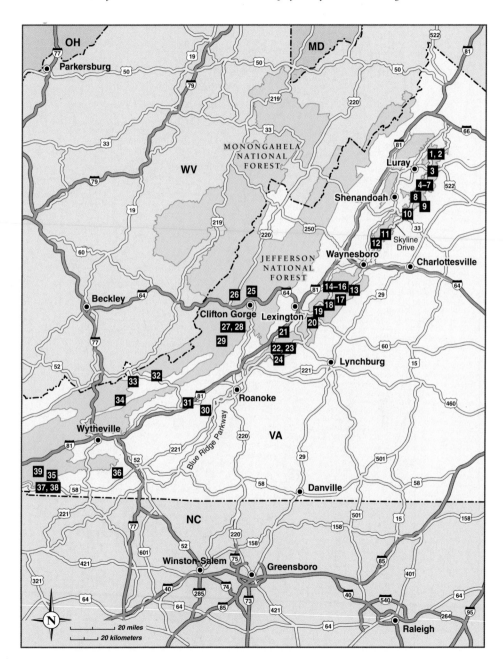

North Carolina Overview Map

See the Table of Contents and individual area maps for keys to numbering below.

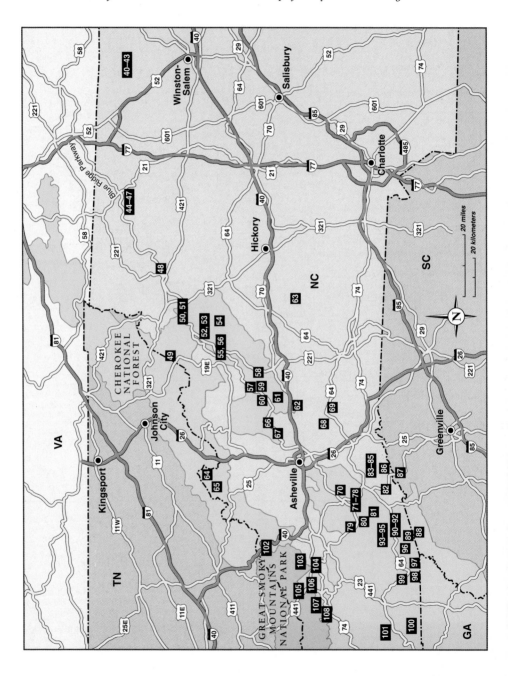

section one

The Basics of Blue Ridge Waterfalls

HIDDEN FALLS *(see Trip 41, page 100)*

About the Blue Ridge

THE BLUE RIDGE MOUNTAINS

Join us on an adventure through the Blue Ridge Mountains. Our fascination with waterfalls brought us here. In our search, we discovered a region rich in natural and human history and encountered compelling physical beauty. It is said that to share a joy is to multiply it. We would like to share the joy of our discoveries with you.

The Blue Ridge Mountains run from southeast Pennsylvania to northwest Georgia. They form the eastern portion of the Appalachian Mountains, the great range that extends 1,600 miles from Quebec Province to Alabama. In Virginia, the Blue Ridge Mountains divide the Piedmont from the Shenandoah Valley. In North Carolina, they form the eastern section of a mountain chain that is more than 75 miles wide and includes the Black Mountains and the Great Smokies.

When seen from a distance, the forested slopes of the Blue Ridge project their bluish tone because of water droplets and gas molecules released into the air by the trees. William Byrd of Virginia was one of the first to note this ever-present blue color in 1728 when he surveyed the boundary between Virginia and North Carolina. Byrd noted that the distant horizon "lookt like Ranges of Blue clouds rising one above another."

STORY OF THE MOUNTAINS

The story of the formation of the Blue Ridge Mountains is not a simple one. These mountains are believed to be among the oldest in the world. Their complicated history helps explain why the mountains exist in their present form. According to plate tectonics, a concept of geologic change, Earth's crust is made up of gigantic, rigid plates of rock that are floating on the hot liquid mantle below. These crusts are always moving—grinding against one another, fusing together, and then breaking apart again.

The process that formed the Appalachians and the Blue Ridge began long ago. Miles beneath the surface of the earth, molten magma slowly solidified into the core of what we now know as the Blue Ridge Mountains. Over time untold, this basement rock folded and uplifted, collided with other landmasses, lay under giant shallow seas, eroded, and once again thrust upward.

The last significant event probably occurred when eastern North America collided with a continental fragment that later became Africa. This collision caused the seafloor to fold, lift, and break apart. The older underlying layer of rock tilted upward and slid over the younger layer, creating the Appalachians. The continents fused and then split again, the Atlantic Ocean filling the void between the separating landmasses.

So, the mountains were formed, but there is more to the story. The rolling mountains we see today were once as jagged and craggy as the Himalayas. The rounded peaks of the Blue Ridge are largely a product of erosion. These forces have sculpted the mountains into peaceful swells shrouded with blue mist. Wind, water, and gravity continue to etch the face of the landscape day by day.

HUMAN HISTORY

The history of the people who have lived in these mountains for centuries is as interesting as the story of the mountains' formation. Archaeological research has found traces of human habitation in this area as early as 8000 BC. Evidence found at various sites throughout the mountains indicates that people have been in the Blue Ridge continuously since that time. American Indian tribes lived off this land before the arrival of Europeans. The first white men were hunters and traders in search of pelts. Tales of savages and other horrors kept many pioneers away. At the same time, the American Indians were battling other tribes. More decimating, however, was the whiskey and smallpox brought by fur traders and pioneers.

The colonists who came here were from hardy stock. They were Scotch-Irish immigrants who had survived hard times in Northern Ireland, and Germans who came to escape the horrible conditions of the Thirty Years' War. They were joined by Englishmen from the coastal regions.

Before the American Revolution, many rebellious colonists entrenched themselves in the mountains. From their mountain strongholds, they fought and defeated the king's men during the Revolution. Later, the Cherokee were their foe. Eventually, the area came entirely under white control.

Because of their physical isolation, these Appalachian pioneers became self-sufficient. Schooling was sporadic. While many of the original settlers could read and write, often these skills gradually slipped away. Christianity was the major influence in their lives. Traveling ministers carried the gospel to the isolated areas and were usually the only outsiders. An old mountain saying, "There's nothing stirring out there but crows and Methodist preachers," hints at the ever-present influence of religion on a people shut off from outside civilization.

Roads were barely passable, when they existed at all. In waves, miners and loggers, enticed by rich ore veins and lush forests, depleted resources and departed. The mountain folk were left as destitute as before, and their land was desecrated. The coming of the automobile, coupled with the increase in road building, brought change to the highlands. Electricity and modern conveniences made life somewhat easier for the mountaineers, but they maintained their self-sufficiency and their unique customs.

With the Blue Ridge Parkway came an interest in the lives of the colorful people who occupy the mountains and valleys of the Blue Ridge. Part of the stated purpose of the Blue Ridge Parkway is to preserve the history and culture of the highlanders.

PLANTS AND ANIMALS

Just as we are intrigued by the history of the mountains and their inhabitants, so are we captivated by the diversity of their natural wonders. This area is one of the most ecologically complex woodlands in North America. Thousands of species have developed here over millions of years of evolution. The dramatic upheavals and shifting that formed the mountains also contributed to the great variety of plant life. Forerunners of rare botanical specimens were deposited in coves created by ancient glaciers.

The abundant rainfall, mild climate, and great variations in elevation make the Blue Ridge a paradise for botanists. Driving from the foothills of the Blue Ridge to the higher elevations, you encounter the same plant life zones that you would find driving from Georgia to New England. Trees vary from the sycamore and river birch typical of Southeastern stream bottoms to spruce and fir forests similar to those found in northern Maine.

Naturalists also find the animal life of the region diverse and plentiful. Hikers may see wild turkeys, beavers, deer, bears, foxes, opossums, rabbits, chipmunks, squirrels, groundhogs, and skunks. Bird-watchers in the Blue Ridge have a great opportunity because a major migratory flyway follows the mountains.

The Blue Ridge Mountains offer incredible seasonal variety. Spring and summer engage visitors with their constant palette of colors, from brilliant to pastel, showcased against a tapestry of greens. Wildflowers, mountain laurel, rhododendron, and flame azalea provide a procession of color that gives way to the spectacular blaze of fall. The muted tones of winter often belie the unpredictability of this season. The rime ice that adorns trees and rocks warns of the chill but provides a magnificent, sparkling picture. The clear, unobstructed panoramas in winter are beyond comparison.

THE BLUE RIDGE PARKWAY

The Blue Ridge Parkway, linking Shenandoah National Park to Great Smoky Mountains National Park, forms the backbone of this marvelous scenic region. The Blue Ridge Parkway provides a platform from which to survey many of the wonders of the entire area. Writer Harley E. Jolley described it as "a road of unlimited horizons, a grand balcony."

The Parkway is also a masterful feat of engineering that has preserved the natural beauty and the cultural heritage of the Southern Highlands. Few of the millions of tourists who travel the scenic road each year have any concept of the hard labor, politics, and dreams that were involved in making it a reality. Considering the countless hardships, adversities, and today's government red tape, it is astonishing that the first rural national parkway in the United States was ever completed.

The Blue Ridge Parkway was designed as a Depression-era project to provide desperately needed jobs for engineers, architects, and landscape architects, as well as for the laborers of the Southern Highlands. The National Park Service archives don't recognize a single originator of the idea. Several people, however, have taken credit. As early as 1909, Colonel Joseph Hyde Pratt, head of the North Carolina Geological Survey, dreamed of a scenic highway through the Blue Ridge Mountains. He even had a short section built before World War I diverted funds and manpower away from the project.

Several historians give credit for the Parkway to Virginia Senator Harry F. Byrd. On an August day in 1933, Byrd was with President Franklin D. Roosevelt,

CATAWBA FALLS *(see Trip 62, page 140)*

who was on an inspection tour of the Civilian Conservation Corps (CCC) in Shenandoah National Park. Roosevelt was very impressed with Shenandoah's Skyline Drive (see the Shenandoah National Park chapter, page 26). Byrd suggested the grandiose scheme of constructing a road to connect Shenandoah National Park and Great Smoky Mountains National Park. Roosevelt was enthusiastic, and the wheels were set in motion. Secretary of the Interior Harold L. Ickes was asked to determine the route.

The problems confronting the Parkway were just beginning, and the project faced incredible obstacles, including debate over the actual path the road would take. Original plans directed the Parkway through North Carolina, Tennessee, and Virginia. Bitter fights between politicians from Tennessee and North Carolina placed Secretary Ickes in a difficult position. Amid great protest from Tennessee officials, he opted for the so-called North Carolina route, stating that he found it to be more scenic and that the Pisgah and Nantahala National Forests would provide a good corridor for the scenic road.

There were many problems obtaining rights-of-way, especially through the Cherokee Indian Reservation, which is the final link to Great Smoky Mountains National Park. After years of negotiations between Cherokee and government officials, the Parkway was routed through the Cherokee Indian Reservation for many of its final miles.

The first rocks of the Parkway were blasted near Cumberland Knob, North Carolina, on September 11, 1935, but it was 52 years before the last 7.5 miles across Grandfather Mountain were completed. The landowners were intensely opposed to the route, and the final right-of-way was not granted until October 22, 1968. This missing link included the Linn Cove Viaduct, said to be one of the most intricate segmental concrete bridges ever constructed. This engineering marvel, which carries vehicles 1,240 feet across the face of Grandfather Mountain, ended the 14-mile detour on US 221. The final section of the Blue Ridge Parkway was completed and dedicated on September 11, 1987.

The Parkway begins at milepost 0 at Rockfish Gap, Virginia, the southern entrance to Shenandoah National Park. For 469 miles, this scenic roadway closely follows the highest ridges of the Southern Appalachians. It ends at milepost 469.1, the entrance to Great Smoky Mountains National Park and the land of the Cherokee. Along the way, the Parkway reaches elevations of more than 6,000 feet, with an average of 3,500 feet. For the first 355 miles, the Parkway closely follows the Blue Ridge in a southwesterly direction. For the remaining 114 miles, it follows the southern end of the imposing Black Mountains and threads through the Craggies, the Pisgahs, and the Balsams.

Traveling the Parkway, visitors are treated to a multitude of panoramic views, varying from dense forests to mile-high mountains. There are plateaus and farmland valleys where early settlers lived. Meadows are lined with split-rail fences and are lush with wildflowers. You will see historic structures such as old farm buildings and homesteads. The cultural sites and the sheer physical beauty preserved here make for a journey rich in history and inspiring scenery.

The one thing that you will not see on your journey is commercial development, although it is rapidly encroaching, especially around Roanoke and Asheville. As a parkway, this road is designed and administered like any other national park, complete with overlooks, exhibits, displays, and interpretive signs. Park rangers work closely with naturalists, agronomists, and environmentalists to protect and restore what lies within the Parkway's domain.

Geographically located within one day's drive of half of the nation's population, the Blue Ridge Parkway is not meant to be a road to somewhere. It is a destination in itself. Millions of visitors come here for the camping facilities, trout-laden streams, picnic grounds, horseback riding, cross-country skiing, hiking trails, and, of course, waterfalls. The Blue Ridge Parkway will lead you to several waterfalls with easy-to-access trailheads at the parking areas and to overlooks directly alongside the road. Watch for the mileposts and enjoy the scenery along this famous drive.

SHENANDOAH NATIONAL PARK

One of the most popular parks in the country, Shenandoah National Park straddles the Blue Ridge at the northern end of the Parkway. This skinny park varies in width from 1 to 13 miles and covers almost 200,000 acres, 95% of which is forest and 40% of which is federally designated wilderness. The 105-mile Skyline Drive rides the ridge, traveling the entire length of the park and providing access to facilities and viewpoints. Shenandoah River and Massanutten Mountain lie to the west; the Piedmont lies to the east.

Shenandoah is an American Indian name. Some say it means "daughter of the stars." Another interpretation is "river of high mountains." Either name is an apt description of the long, narrow park on the crest of the mountains. A trip through Shenandoah along Skyline Drive is a ride across the top of Virginia.

Two federal projects were instrumental in the development of Shenandoah National Park, even before it was officially established. One was Skyline Drive, which was planned to generate jobs in the economically depressed area. President Herbert Hoover authorized the use of drought-relief funds for its construction, which began in 1931. The second was the Civilian Conservation Corps, which contributed a great deal to Shenandoah. Following the CCC's creation in 1933, 10 camps were established in the area. The Corps' men were given responsibility for firefighting, erosion control, trail and road construction, infrastructure such as telephone and water service, and planting trees and bushes in open areas and on the roadside along the entire Skyline Drive.

In 1926 Congress approved Shenandoah as a site for a large Southern national park. However, while federal funds had been used to build Skyline Drive and fund CCC projects in the area, no federal monies were appropriated for building the park. Western parks had been established on federal land, but populated private lands had never before been designated for a park. Consequently, there was no precedent for such a purchase, which had to be made with donated funds.

The campaign to create and fund the park involved the untiring efforts of thousands of private citizens, as well as many employees of the state of Virginia. Senator Byrd was an enthusiastic supporter. A total of $1.3 million was pledged by Virginia's residents, and the state legislature added another $1 million. A great deal of partisan lobbying went into the site selection for the park. George Freeman Pollock, an entrepreneur and owner of the Skyland Resort in northern Virginia, was influential in the selection. His enthusiasm and energy were tremendous assets in the effort to have the final site chosen. Finally, after years of fights and lawsuits, the state of Virginia had clear title to more than 250 square miles of the Blue Ridge Mountains. Virginia presented this land to

GAUGE ROCK CASCADES *(see Trip 9, page 42)*

the United States on December 12, 1935. President Franklin Roosevelt dedicated the park on July 3, 1936.

Entrance stations at four points split the park into north, central, and south districts. The North District of the park is close to Washington, D.C., and many visitors enter there. The Central District contains the park's primary overnight lodging accommodations (and many of its waterfalls). The South District offers much of the beautiful backcountry for which Shenandoah is known. Some facilities are open year-round, but the majority operate mid-May–late October.

The park includes 500 miles of hiking trails, varying in length from leg stretchers to 101 miles of the Appalachian Trail, and the waterfall hikes are some of the most popular. Skyline Drive runs roughly parallel to the Appalachian Trail, and many hikers consider this portion of the Appalachian Trail to be one of the most beautiful. Additionally, there is enough backcountry to keep backpackers busy for a long while.

The forest, primarily oak and hickory, is an ecosystem with many life-forms. The flora includes rose azaleas, lady's slipper orchids, jack-in-the-pulpits, interrupted ferns, and more than 1,300 other plants. Animal life abounds in the park as well. White-tailed deer (which visitors see frequently), wild turkeys, and black bears call the park home. Of the 200 species of birds recorded in the park, you may see some of the permanent residents such as ruffed grouse, barred owls, and woodpeckers.

Often called a gentle wilderness, Shenandoah National Park offers many unique areas. One of the most unusual is the large plateau known as Big Meadows, located at an elevation of 3,500 feet. Big Meadows has the greatest variety of plant life in the park, with at least 300 species, as well as a wide variety of animal life. At Big Meadows, you'll find a lodge and campground, as well as a gift shop, a camp store, a gas station, and several of the waterfall trailheads.

Other areas of the park offer their own unrivaled features. At Big Devils Stairs, you can find some of the oldest trees, which are inaccessible to timbering. Hawksbill, at 4,051 feet, is the highest point in the park and contains remnant red-spruce and balsam-fir forests. Painted trilliums await at Laurel Prong.

The park features two visitor centers, an information center, five campgrounds, and seven picnic areas. The park does have an entrance fee, which is good for seven days. Yearly passes are also available.

GREAT SMOKY MOUNTAINS NATIONAL PARK

Located at the southern end of the Blue Ridge Parkway, Great Smoky Mountains National Park is filled with majestic mountains; hiking trails; beautiful camp-sites; and rivers for fishing, swimming, and tubing.

The Great Smoky Mountains are part of the Blue Ridge Mountains, and the Cherokee called the area *Shaconage,* or "place of blue smoke." The bluish mist that pervades the valleys and hovers over the Blue Ridge Mountains is even more visible in the Smokies, creating a mysterious and eerie hue.

The Cherokee people were the first inhabitants of the Great Smoky Mountains. While geologists have developed theories about how the moun-tains were formed, the Cherokee have another version. Legend has it that a great buzzard was sent down from the sky to find a dry place for everyone to live. Over Cherokee land, the buzzard became very weary and dropped close to the earth. His beating wings struck the soft earth, forming the mountains and valleys and creating the tribe's homeland.

The Smokies were seen by some for their timber value more so than their scenic worth. Much of what became the park was logged. A St. Louis librarian named Horace Kephart was one of the first to recognize the value of the Great Smoky Mountains. He came to the Great Smokies in 1904 to recover from ill health and grew to love the mountains. Appalled by the wide-scale decimation of the land, Kephart worked doggedly for years to have the Smokies preserved as a national park. In *Our Southern Highlands,* he wrote of his years in Deep Creek, Hazel Creek, and Bryson City. His sensitive writing helped alert the public to the fact that the mountains were being destroyed and its residents' way of life overlooked.

In 1923, Mr. and Mrs. Willis P. Davis and Colonel David Chapman of Knoxville, Tennessee, formed the Great Smoky Mountains Conservation Associa-tion. Under the leadership of Colonel Chapman, and with the influence of others such as Kephart, groups in North Carolina and Tennessee began to raise money to buy the land. Businessman and philanthropist John D. Rockefeller contributed $5 million to the cause. With the help of all these contributors, Great Smoky Mountains National Park was established on June 15, 1934.

Like Shenandoah, it incorporated private land, which had to be pur-chased from individuals, much by eminent domain. Once again, there were many questions concerning titles and rights-of-way. Finally, President Franklin Roosevelt officially dedicated the park on September 2, 1940.

The park sits astride the border of North Carolina and Tennessee. Elevations range from 840 feet at the mouth of Abrams Creek to 6,642 feet at Clingmans Dome. There are more than 900 miles of trails and footpaths, including 70 miles of the Appalachian Trail. These pathways thread through the park, leading to coves, balds, and rushing streams, as well as dozens of waterfalls. This book includes several waterfall hikes accessed from Bryson City and Cherokee.

From the Blue Ridge Parkway on the North Carolina side of the park, the first stop is the Oconaluftee Visitor Center, which is open year-round. Here, you can get park information and literature about the Smokies. Adjacent to the visitor center is the Mountain Farm Museum, an exhibit that shows how the mountains' first settlers lived. Just north of the visitor center on Newfound Gap Road, Mingus Mill, a large, water-powered gristmill, grinds corn daily from mid-March to October.

"Always clear and fragrant," wrote Kephart about the forests of the Smokies, and so they are. The park is a sanctuary, preserving some of the world's finest examples of temperate deciduous forest. More than 130 species of trees grow in the Smokies. Broadleaf trees dominate in the coves, and conifer forests cover the crests at the highest elevations. This is the largest remaining virgin forest of the eastern American wilderness, covering an estimated 100,000 acres, or 20% of the park. Of the old-growth forest that remains in the eastern United States, 90% lies within Great Smoky Mountains National Park.

The park encompasses nearly 800 square miles. Within its boundaries lies a wealth of natural wonders. The annual rainfall in the park is more than 85 inches at the higher elevations, equivalent to that in a rainforest. This abundant rainfall and the fertile soil have encouraged the development of a world-renowned variety of flora, with more than 1,500 kinds of flowering plants. Many plants in the higher elevations are more typical of New England than of the southeastern United States.

An additional attraction is the diversity of animal life. There are more than 400 species of animals, including 200 species of birds. The park is this country's salamander capital, with 30 species. There are at least 60 species of mammals, including bears, deer, and wild boars. The wild boars, however, are not a native species and pose a threat to the ecosystem. Their wallowing behavior destroys soil-level plant life, including rare species, and even the nests and eggs of ground-nesting birds. Park officials are working to remove these animals.

WATERFALLS

Of all the many treasures to be found in these two national parks and along the Parkway, the most precious are the water resources. The Blue Ridge is laced with miles upon miles of rivers and streams. In essence, the mountains were molded by the force of water, and water continues to sculpt the valleys and ridges. The nature and personality of the Blue Ridge Mountains are intrinsically tied to the mystery, magic, and movement of water.

We came to research the waterfalls of the Blue Ridge; we learned about the complex interrelationship between modern civilization and nature. Eons of evolution determined the type of plant and animal life that would survive in this region. Aboriginals dwelled here for centuries, and settlers from far and wide became hardy Appalachian pioneers. Today, ecological and cultural sights abound on the waterfall trails of the Blue Ridge Mountains.

We came to see the waterfalls, and we found the Blue Ridge Parkway, that undulating ribbon of highway that connects two national parks. The road exists as a monument to those who were committed to providing us all with a view from the mountaintops.

We came to see the waterfalls, and we discovered Shenandoah National Park and Great Smoky Mountains National Park. These parks are being preserved as the crown jewels of the Southern Appalachians.

We came to see the waterfalls, and we took away a sense of the mystery and majesty of the mountains. Come and see the waterfalls of the Blue Ridge yourself. Enjoy the peace that the mountains offer. Take a moment to consider the abundant beauty at hand and the farsighted wisdom of preserving all of this for future generations.

section two

Virginia Waterfalls

APPLE ORCHARD FALLS *(see Trip 22, page 64)*

Shenandoah National Park

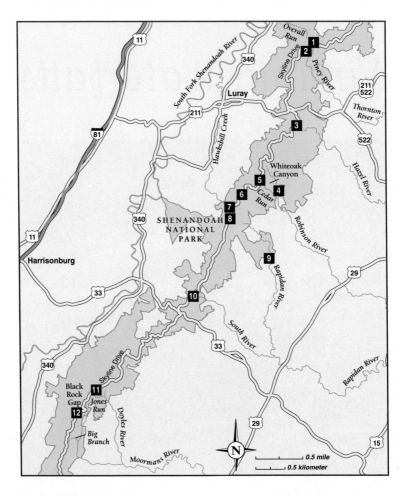

1 OVERALL RUN FALLS AND TWIN FALLS
[6.8-mile out-and-back, strenuous]

Overall Run is Shenandoah's highest falls. The cataract is complemented with a grand vista and a warm-up fall along the way. Start with a pleasant mountain-top stroll on the Appalachian Trail, and wend your way down the slopes of Hogback Mountain, crossing many flats. Pass wide Twin Falls, and then come to Big Falls. From a rocky precipice, you can see the nearby cataract and a whole lot more in the distance.

From the parking area, join the Appalachian Trail and head south. Gently climb through lovely fern-carpeted woodland, passing a few rock outcrops. At 0.4 mile, turn right onto the Tuscarora–Overall Run Trail. Stroll downward. Rock and wood erosion bars cross the trail and form steps. Make a couple of switch-backs before coming to another trail junction at 1.1 miles. Here, meet a connector to the Traces Nature Trail. You aren't far from Mathews Arm Campground, a fine base camp to explore the falls of Shenandoah.

Turn right, staying on the Tuscarora–Overall Run Trail. Stairstep down Hogback Mountain. At 1.6 miles, hop over uppermost Overall Run. This trickling branch increases hope that a waterfall awaits at the end of this dry hike. The adjacent high-elevation flats seem to attract bears, which we've seen multiple times around this area.

At 2.9 miles, the trail intersects Mathews Arm Trail. Keep right. Walk just a short distance and come to another concrete signpost. Here, pass the now aban-doned section of Mathews Arm Trail. At this point you may be wondering where the falls are getting their water. The Tuscarora–Overall Run Trail answers the question and turns left toward Overall Run on wood and earth steps. Reach the first cataract, Twin Falls, at 3.1 miles. A side trail leads left to Twin Falls and a rock outcrop where you can view it. Overall Run is split by a large boulder, forcing the water to divide, resulting in two streams dropping 29 feet.

Keep astride the canyon, passing through laurel–oak woods. Tempting outcrops lure you to the edge of the valley. Come to a wide-open cliff at 3.4 miles. The world opens beyond. To your left Big Falls tumbles 93 feet over a huge rock face into the gorge below. More rock forms a wall on the far side of the falls. The Overall Run canyon plunges below. It's a long way down there!

The canyon maw divulges Page Valley and Massanutten Mountain in the background. In the distance you can see West Virginia and the Alleghenies . . . a great waterfall and a great view.

DIRECTIONS The hike starts at the parking area just south of the Hogback Mountain Overlook, milepost 21.1 on Skyline Drive. To reach the trailhead from the Thornton Gap entrance station, take Skyline Drive north for 10.4 miles to the parking area on the west side of Skyline Drive, just before Hogback Mountain Overlook.

GPS TRAILHEAD COORDINATES 38.761267, -78.282317

OVERALL RUN FALLS

2 PINEY RIVER FALLS
[6.8-mile out-and-back, moderate–strenuous]

Piney River Falls is one of the least-visited cataracts at Shenandoah, and we're flummoxed about why. The trailside scenery meets high Shenandoah standards, and the falls are a worthy destination. Start your hike at the back of the field between Skyline Drive and the parking area across from the old Civilian Conservation Corps camp building. Look for the concrete post marked PINEY BRANCH TRAIL. Hike through black locust trees taking over an old pasture. Almost one-third of the land within Shenandoah National Park was once field, pasture, or meadow—treeless. At 0.1 mile intersect the Appalachian Trail and continue straight on a track much fainter than the AT. Just ahead, cross a grassy lane, also growing up with trees. Note the apple trees.

The Piney Branch Trail winds downhill in very gentle switchbacks. Come to the upper reaches of the Piney River at mile 1.3. Big boulders line the small river, and the grassy area beside the stream makes for a good sitting spot. Curve right, away from Piney River. Spring-fed creeklets cross the rocky path ahead. Park personnel did an outstanding job of keeping a dry track in this mushy area.

Meet the Pole Bridge Link Trail at 1.5 miles. Turn right, staying with the now narrower and even less-used section of the Piney Branch Trail. Wildflowers thrive in the Piney River Valley. The mountain laurel–lined path follows an old road on a slight downgrade. The gorge of Piney River cuts ever deeper to your right. At mile 2.0, the old road continues straight, but the Piney Branch Trail veers right and follows another old road. At 2.7 miles, the trail nears the Piney River. A spur trail leads right to the riverside and a nice picnic spot. Stay straight here, going deeper into the valley.

Cross the Piney River at 3.0 miles. This is a rock hop at normal flows, but it takes a little footwork. Another method is to simply shed your shoes and socks and walk through the water with a stout stick as an aid. At lower levels, this crossing will be a breeze. You are now on the southern side of the river, and the falls are only 0.4 mile distant. Watch and listen for other cascades along Piney River while making your way downstream. Cove hardwoods of yellow birch, black birch, red maple, and basswood shade the frothing watercourse.

PINEY RIVER FALLS

Stumble through river rubble, flood-strewn rocks from high-water events. Ferns spread wide beside rock outcrops, and sycamores find their place amid the rocks and water. Pass two house-size rock bluffs on your right at mile 3.2. A hard-to-reach falls spills to your left. This part of the gorge is rugged. Begin listening for Piney River Falls, which are only 0.2 mile away. At mile 3.4, turn left on a side trail leading to the cataract. Piney River Falls is a 25-foot tiered cascade that flows over mossy rock into a deep and wide pool. Rock slabs border much of the drop and make for good observation locales. It's a good place to cool off after a hot hike, so relax a spell.

DIRECTIONS From the Thornton Gap entrance of the park, take Skyline Drive north for 9.4 miles to the old Civilian Conservation Corps building in the upper Piney River area. The entrance road is on your right at milepost 22.1, just north of the turn to Mathews Arm Campground on the left. Park in the designated visitor parking area across from the CCC building. The Piney Branch Trail starts between the parking area and Skyline Drive.

GPS TRAILHEAD COORDINATES 38.750500, -78.292317

3 HAZEL FALLS
[5.2-mile out-and-back, moderate]

This waterfall walk takes you into Hazel Country, a heavily settled area before Shenandoah National Park was formed. The route traverses hills and hollows to reach the banks of the Hazel River, where a rock indentation forms a natural shelter, a cave of sorts, beside an alluring waterfall, all located within a deep stone amphitheater. The difficulty of this hike is hard to rate: The first 2.4-mile portion is an easy stroll on old settler roads, but the last 0.3-mile trek to the falls and cave is on a steep footpath. Though rugged, this section has been upgraded by the National Park Service; it was once an eroded user-created mess of a path.

Leave Skyline Drive on the Hazel Mountain Trail. At 0.4 mile, veer right, still on the Hazel Mountain Trail, as the Buck Ridge Trail drops left. Striped maples crowd the path and form a dense canopy overhead. The trail bears left, levels out, and crosses several small spring-fed branches dribbling off Buck

HAZEL FALLS

Ridge. Sidle alongside the Hazel River at mile 1.0. The valley spreads wide into a cove, which was farmland long ago.

. Turn left on White Rocks Trail at mile 1.6. The path ascends slightly, leaving Hazel River, and then levels out along an old road shaded by tulip trees and maples. Large boulders are strewn about the forest, which morphs to pine and chestnut oak as the trail tops out on the ridge. Wild azaleas bloom in May. An aquatic symphony drifts from below. Come to a trail junction at mile 2.4. White Rocks Trail continues forward, while Cave–Falls Trail veers right. Follow Cave–Falls Trail downhill, the steep dive mitigated by stone steps.

Reach Hazel River at 2.5 miles. Notice the peeling trunks of the many yellow birches. Turn right, following the footpath upstream. Pass a sizable trailside tulip tree as you dance between boulders. Reach the rock shelter on your right just before the waterfall; the rock indentation lies at the base of a huge, granite bluff—quite a sturdy roof. The cave is about 10 feet deep, 25 feet wide, and 7 feet high. It gets a little deeper in one spot. A natural rock amphitheater envelops the scene. Hazel Falls slices about 25 feet down a slender chute into a stony punch bowl and forms the centerpiece of this picturesque mountain mosaic.

DIRECTIONS The trailhead and parking area are located on the east side of milepost 33.5 of Skyline Drive, Meadow Spring. It can be accessed by driving south for 2 miles from Shenandoah National Park's Thornton Gap entrance on Skyline Drive.

GPS TRAILHEAD COORDINATES 38.637500, -78.314083

4 WATERFALLS OF WHITEOAK CANYON
[5.4-mile out-and-back, strenuous]

It's hard to keep track of all the falls at Whiteoak Canyon. There are six numbered falls. The count starts from the crest of the Blue Ridge and Skyline Drive and ends at the base of the canyon. To confuse matters, this hike starts at the bottom of Whiteoak Run and heads upstream, which is the best way to see all the falls in the fewest miles hiked. *Note:* Beware of the warm-weather weekend crowds. We highly suggest heading to a different waterfall during those times.

Leave the parking area on a trail easement through private property, reaching Cedar Run. At this point, the streambed is often dry, though Cedar Run may be flowing farther upstream. Span Cedar Run on a metal bridge. Beech, sycamore, black birch, and magnolia trees shade the track. When you reach the Cedar Run Trail junction at 0.2 mile, veer right, staying on Whiteoak Canyon Trail. Bridge Whiteoak Run, a rocky river if there ever was one, and gently ascend the creek bank. Sycamores overhang the scenic stream. Note the rock walls and piles, evidence that this area was once cultivated.

Pass the junction with the Whiteoak–Cedar Run Link Trail at 0.8 mile. Stay on the east bank of Whiteoak Run, and enter a rock garden. The canyon closes, and the stream gathers in deep pools. The path becomes rockier and steeper. Rock-hop Tims River, which has falls of its own, on your right. Just beyond this crossing, close in on Lower Whiteoak Falls (number 6) at 1.4 miles. A short trail leads left to the precipitous two-tiered, 60-foot cataract, which spills over an open rock face. The uppermost falls, this hike's turnaround point, is the canyon's tallest at 86 feet. The ones in between—which are hard to count because it is indiscernible where they start or stop—purportedly range from 45 to 65 feet each.

The main trail switchbacks, meandering far from the stream. The area can be confusing, as erosive user-created trails continue straight up the canyon. Climb sharply along the base of a bluff in pines, well above the stream, sometimes traversing open rock. In places, steps have been chiseled into this bare stone. At 1.7 miles, come to a cedar tree that mans a rock-slab overlook into the canyon. Catch glimpses of the crashing falls below and the lands beyond the canyon. The stream and path come together again by 1.9 miles. This is where the numbered falls get confusing. Simply enjoy the cataracts and leave the counting to others.

Begin a pattern of coming to a falls and then switchbacking away and uphill to the base of another. Huge walls rise beyond the stream. Pass an overhanging boulder on your right at 2.3 miles. Keep climbing through a wonderment of rock and water, where pools and cascades beckon you off the trail and to Whiteoak Run. As you continue uphill, a melding of stone and concrete makes the pathway more hiker-friendly. A side trail leads left to the base of Whiteoak Falls (number 1) at 2.5 miles. The main trail switchbacks to the right and passes a concrete trail marker indicating the halfway point of the Whiteoak Canyon Trail, with a warning for hikers that no shuttle is available at the bottom of the canyon. Apparently, hikers have walked Whiteoak Canyon Trail from Skyline Drive and decided that they could not walk back up.

Come to a rock observation point for Whiteoak Falls (number 1) at 2.7 miles. You are well above the falls on a large slab. This is the second-highest falls in the park at 86 feet. It slides over bare rock in multiple stages bordered by hardwoods. Rest and enjoy these falls and the good view into the canyon below. On your return trip, try to count them. After all, Whiteoak Run has more falls per mile than any other stream in the park.

> **DIRECTIONS**　From the town of Madison, Virginia, on US 29 north of Char-
> lottesville and south of Culpeper, drive north on VA 231 for 5 miles to VA 670.
> Turn left on VA 670 and follow it for 5 miles to VA 643. Turn right on VA 643 and
> follow it for less than a mile to VA 600. Turn left on VA 600 and follow it for
> 3.7 miles to Berry Hollow. The trailhead is in the back of the far parking area,
> which will be on your right.

> **GPS TRAILHEAD COORDINATES**　38.539133, -78.348100

5 CEDAR RUN FALLS
[3.4-mile out-and-back, strenuous]

This hike leads you into rugged upper Cedar Run Canyon. The trail down to the main falls is steep. However, aquatic rewards are many along the way—you pass innumerable cascades spilling down the narrow, boulder-laden gorge, a wild place deserving of national park protection. Your trip to the cascades will be slow, as you will need to watch your footing and stop often to admire the scenery. *Note:* This hike can be busy on warm-weather weekends.

Leave grassy Hawksbill Gap to enter tall hardwoods on Cedar Run Trail. Immediately come to a four-way trail junction. Keep straight, descending, still on Cedar Run Trail. The Skyland–Big Meadows Horse Trail leaves left and right. Pass a rock outcrop often used as a relaxing locale for those returning up Cedar Run Canyon. The trail grade drops sharply in a thick forest alongside the upper reaches of Cedar Run. The white noise of cold mountain water serenades you all the way to the falls.

A northern hardwood forest of cherry, witch hazel, sugar maple, and large oak trees rises from the stony woods. Despite elaborate trail work by the

CEDAR RUN FALLS

National Park Service, the path remains very rocky. Take your time and carefully plant your feet—a rolled ankle is possible here. Sturdy boots and trekking poles will make this waterfall hike more palatable. On the plus side, the plethora of boulders provides ample resting spots on your return trip.

Cedar Run picks up steam on its drop, falling in multiple incarnations of moving water. A side branch crosses the trail, forming a cascade of its own. At 0.6 mile, step onto a wide rock, facing a cascade to your right. Cedar Run descends 20 feet in a fan pattern and then crashes onto the rock atop which you are standing. Beyond this waterfall, the trail drops steeply alongside a stairstep cataract to your right and a rocky bluff to your left. At 0.9 mile, enjoy a brief interlude of level, relatively rockless pathway. Then the trail resumes, diving headlong into a procession of stone, and passes another waterslide-type pour-over. At other times, monstrous midstream boulders nearly obscure the water as it seeks gravity's level. At 1.1 miles, away from the stream, rock ramparts rise from the trees, forming canyon walls that echo and redouble the sounds of moving water.

At 1.3 miles, on the far side of the trail, a tributary stream adds its flow in a waterslide. A deep pool with brook trout forms on Cedar Run just below this tributary. The clash of water and rock remains relentless. At 1.4 miles, pass another cliff line. At 1.5 miles, the trail comes to a big, alluring pool below a two-tiered cascade. You have reached the crossing of Cedar Run. This is usually a rock hop; however, it can be a wet crossing at high water.

You are now on the right bank heading downstream. Yet the trail goes uphill, passing a feeder stream trickling in from your right. Cedar Run Trail then descends a set of stone steps to the base of Cedar Run Falls at 1.7 miles. The water spills down a slick rock face and lands in a deep and clear plunge pool, and then it drops again in whitewater froth charging through a narrow slot canyon.

Many large boulders make relaxing observation points at this mid-falls area. Half Mile Cliff rises on the far side of the falls. You can go a bit farther downstream to enjoy the lower segment of Cedar Run Falls. It has a deep plunge pool at the base of the slot canyon. You will be thinking of reasons to hang out down here, as the hike back is steep. Pace yourself, and use those trailside boulders to catch your breath.

DIRECTIONS The Hawksbill Gap trailhead is located at milepost 45.6 on Skyline Drive, 14 miles south of the Thornton Gap entrance to Shenandoah National Park. Cedar Run Trail starts behind the gravel parking area on the east side of Skyline Drive.

GPS TRAILHEAD COORDINATES 38.556567, -78.386567

6 DARK HOLLOW FALLS AND ROSE RIVER FALLS
[4.0-mile loop, moderate]

This loop hike is the best way to bag both Dark Hollow Falls and Rose River Falls. Most visitors reach Dark Hollow Falls via Skyline Drive. You will begin your trek on Rose River Fire Road and gently descend to reach the lower Dark Hollow Falls Trail. Make the worthwhile 0.2-mile ascent to reach Dark Hollow Falls. Next, follow the Rose River Loop Trail downstream along Hogcamp Branch, passing numerous cascades along what is arguably the prettiest stream in Shenandoah National Park. Bridge Hogcamp Branch, and then pass the tailings of an old copper mine. Beyond here, the hike ascends the upper Rose River, passing Rose River Falls before returning to the trailhead.

Pick up the gated Rose River Fire Road on the east side of Skyline Drive. Walk just a few feet down Rose River Fire Road and reach an intersection. The Skyland–Big Meadows Horse Trail crosses the fire road. Keep straight on Rose River Fire Road, descending along the gravel track in a maple- and white oak–dominated hardwood forest. Small rills flow off Big Meadows above and then pass under the fire road via a culvert. The track levels out among locust trees, land once farmed. Pass the Cave Cemetery on your right, atop a grassy hill, at 0.5 mile.

Reach the junction with Dark Hollow Falls Trail at a bridge over Hogcamp Branch at 1.0 mile. Check out the 30-foot fall just above the bridge. A ribbon of frothing whitewater slices through a rock outcrop partially covered in moss. Turn right and head up Dark Hollow Falls Trail. More falls tumble down as you ascend. However, you will know Dark Hollow Falls. It makes a wide drop and then gathers to tumble down three more tiers, a total descent of 70 feet. In summer, the base of the falls will be crowded, as most everyone has come from Skyline Drive on the Dark Hollow Falls Trail.

Return to Rose River Fire Road and cross the bridge, leaving the crowds behind. Just beyond here, Rose River Loop Trail angles left and downhill along Hogcamp Branch. Young hardwoods are replacing adelgid-killed hemlocks and, for now, Dark Hollow is dark no more. Hogcamp Branch puts on a scenic display while stairstepping down to meet Rose River, falling and crashing in every type of fall, slide, cataract, and cascade, one tumbler after another, to gather in surprisingly deep pools, only to fall yet again. This is truly national park–level scenery.

At 2.0 miles, pass an open rock slab on the creek that lures in hikers. A deep pool lies at the base of the slab. At 2.2 miles, reach a bridge spanning Hogcamp Branch. The steel span arches well over and above Hogcamp Branch. Rose River Loop then rock-hops a small stream. Reach the tailings of an old copper mine, with a path leading to the top of the tailings, back against a big bluff. Notice the stone- and ironworks at the mine. This mine was opened in the early 1900s but proved unprofitable, and the shafts were filled. Keep downhill to reach a signpost near a large wooded flat. Turn left here and head upstream along Rose River, which is crashing to your right, giving Hogcamp Branch a run for its scenic money.

DARK HOLLOW FALLS

Rose River Loop Trail leaves the river, climbing sharply in a ferny forest, only to return at Rose River Falls at 2.8 miles. Here, the watercourse drops over a rock ledge about 30 feet, spreading out before reaching a pool. A spur trail leads downstream to a vista at lower Rose River Falls, which drops again directly over a second ledge and out of sight from the viewing spot, making a splash into a large pool.

Beyond the falls, ascend a perched valley under thriving hardwoods such as yellow birch and basswood. Reach another concrete signpost when meeting an old roadbed at 3.1 miles. Turn left here on a now wide trail, leaving the river. Rise into drier, oak-dominated woods to meet the Skyland–Big Meadows Horse Trail at 3.6 miles. Stay left here, as the two trails run in conjunction, mostly climbing to reach Rose River Fire Road. It is but a few steps to Skyline Drive from here. Complete your loop at 4.0 miles.

DIRECTIONS The Rose River Fire Road starts on the east side of Skyline Drive, just north of Fishers Gap Overlook, at milepost 49.4. Parking is on the west side of the drive. The overlook is on a short spur loop that leaves Skyline Drive. Rose River Fire Road starts across Skyline Drive from the overlook's north end. From the Swift Run Gap entrance, it is 16.1 miles to Fishers Gap Overlook.

GPS TRAILHEAD COORDINATES 38.533567, -78.420783

7 LEWIS SPRING FALLS
[3.4-mile loop, moderate]

Don't forget to bring your camera, so you can capture the visual features along this high-country waterfall walk. The loop takes place near the busy Big Meadows area, with its park lodge, visitor center, ranger station, and campground. Thus, this circuit gets traffic, but deservedly so. Leave the parking area near Tanner Ridge Overlook and head down Lewis Spring Service Road to reach the Appalachian Trail (AT). Walk northbound on the AT, climbing to Blackrock and its stellar views. From there, the hike passes more interesting rock features and then joins Lewis Falls Trail, where it descends to a loud and dramatic falls. Lewis Spring Falls is one of the highest-elevation falls at Shenandoah.

The start can be confusing. Leave the little parking area just north of the Tanner Ridge Overlook. Walk a few yards north along Skyline Drive to reach Lewis Spring Service Road. Pass around a chain gate, and then head downhill on a gravel track bordered by a stunted high-country forest of haw, fire cherry, and maple reclaiming former fields. Look for apple, birch, and locust trees too. The blue-blazed track crosses the yellow-blazed Tanners Ridge Horse Trail and continues descending.

At 0.2 mile, reach the AT. Turn right here, heading northbound for Big Meadows Lodge. Lewis Spring is just below this intersection. Begin working uphill in hardwoods mixed with rocks, pines, and even a preserved hemlock or two. The well-used path features stonework to keep the trail from sloping. At 0.7 mile, reach a spur trail leading right to Blackrock. Turn right and make the 0.1-mile climb to the outcrop, at 3,720 feet. Along the way, see if you can find a few red spruce trees. In winter, the evergreens are easy to spot among the barren hardwoods. Mountain ash clings to the crags of Blackrock. The spiny rock protrusion opens to the west, where you can see the towns of Stanley and Luray in

Page Valley, especially the high peaks of the park's north district, amid the 180-degree view to the southwest and northwest. Below, the tops of oak trees seem close enough to touch. When the leaves are off, the AT can be seen below.

Return to the AT, cruising along the base of Blackrock. Ahead, pass below Big Meadows Lodge before meeting Lewis Falls Trail at 1.3 miles. Here, turn acutely left on Lewis Falls Trail into lush woods with a fern-filled understory. Keep south along the western escarpment of the mountain. Curve onto a south-west-facing slope, with mountain laurels and pines joining the sturdy oaks. Outcrops along the trail provide views into the hollow of upper Hawksbill Creek.

Reach another junction at 2.5 miles. Here, a spur trail leads right to an outcrop with a view into the valley below and lands beyond. Massanutten Mountain forms a backdrop. The main spur path crosses wide and rocky Hawksbill Creek and then curves beyond a precipice. A guardrail guides you the last bit to a rock-walled observation point. Here, you can look down at the 81-foot falls spilling over the rock face, crashing into rocks and then splashing

LEWIS SPRING FALLS

out of sight. There is no safe way to reach the base of the falls, so do not endanger others by trying it and getting hurt.

Backtrack to Lewis Falls Trail and begin a switchback-filled ascent along upper Hawksbill Creek, drifting into rich waterside woods and drier pine-oak forest away from the stream. Join an old roadbed, and then pass the actual Lewis Spring, which is housed in a rock-and-wood structure with a visible outflow. Just ahead, reach the AT again, at 3.2 miles. To your right is another boxed spring. From here, keep straight on the gravel road, backtracking to the trailhead.

DIRECTIONS The parking area for Lewis Spring Service Road is at mile 51.4 on Skyline Drive. This parking area is sandwiched between Big Meadows' south entrance and Tanners Ridge Overlook, on the west side of the road. The trailhead is 19.9 miles south of the Shenandoah National Park's Thornton Gap entrance station.

GPS TRAILHEAD COORDINATES 38.516933, -78.442317

8 BIG ROCK FALLS
[3.0-mile round-trip, moderate]

The plunge pool of Big Rock Falls was a favorite fishing hole for President Herbert Hoover (1929–1933), as it was near his retreat in what is now Shenandoah National Park. This first presidential refuge, known as Camp Rapidan, is only 0.4 mile beyond Big Rock Falls. You should add the extra distance to see this preserved locale, where President Hoover escaped the hot summers of Washington, D.C., during the pre–air-conditioning days. The president also hosted world leaders at Camp Rapidan. The site is chock-full of interpretive information.

Start the waterfall hike at Milam Gap on Skyline Drive, heading east on the Mill Prong Trail to immediately cross the Appalachian Trail. Here, delve into open, ferny forest, and then hop wide, shallow, and rocky Mill Prong at 0.6 mile. Descend farther into the Mill Prong vale, stepping over a side stream before meeting the Mill Prong Horse Trail at 1.1 miles. You'll stay straight with the Mill Prong Trail on a level but rocky section before switchbacking down to come alongside Big Rock Falls at 1.5 miles, a descent of around 600 feet. Here, find a wide slide cascade flowing white into a clear plunge pool. A large rock

Big Rock Falls

at the top of the 14-foot falls inspires the name. Hoover's Rapidan Camp is less than a half mile away, enhancing the trek.

DIRECTIONS From Harrisonburg, Virginia, take US 33 east 23 miles to Shenandoah National Park and Swift Run Gap. Turn north on Skyline Drive and follow it for 12.7 miles to the Milam Gap trailhead, at milepost 52.8, on the west side of Skyline Drive. The hike starts on the east side of Skyline Drive.

GPS TRAILHEAD COORDINATES 38.500306, -78.445639

9 FALLS OF THE STAUNTON RIVER
[2.2-mile round-trip, easy]

This hike ventures to two overlooked falls on the Staunton River, coursing down the east slope of the Blue Ridge in Shenandoah National Park. The hike starts low and stays low, ranging from 1,100 feet to 1,400 feet with no fords, making it a preferred winter waterfall trek.

Start on the wide Graves Mill Trail, heading upstream along the left-hand bank of the rocky, sizable, and scenic Rapidan River. The walking is easy. At

0.5 mile, split left on the Staunton River Trail. At 0.6 mile, scramble downhill to your first waterfall, just upstream of a USGS water-monitoring station. You can see it from the trail above or walk down to its base and pool. This one—Gauge Rock Cascades—pours about 20 feet over a stone face in multiple rivulets. The rock face is open to the sun above. Continuing uptrail, wander through former farmland now grown to forest while the Staunton River flows around small islands. Look for stone fences, rock piles, and other evidence of human habitation. At 1.1 miles, the trail leads past 20-foot Jitterbug Falls, so named for its twisting, turning course, as it froths white into a large plunge pool.

DIRECTIONS From Madison, Virginia, on the east side of Shenandoah National Park, take US 29 south for 2 miles to turn right onto VA 230 west. Follow VA 230 for 3.7 miles to turn right onto VA 662. Follow VA 662 for 5.3 miles, then stay right on Graves Mill Road, still on VA 662. Follow Graves Mill Road for 1.3 miles to reach the trailhead. Do not block the gate.

GPS TRAILHEAD COORDINATES 38.436944, -78.366944

JITTERBUG FALLS

10 SOUTH RIVER FALLS

[4.2-mile out-and-back, moderate]

The valley of upper South River is quite scenic, with its rich wildflower habitat, northern hardwoods, and two impressive perches to view South River Falls dropping 83 feet over a rock face. Go farther and enjoy the setting from the base of the falls. You will have to fight the earth's tug on your climb out of the South River watershed, back to the former mountaintop pastureland, but the falls are worth the scramble.

Take South River Falls Trail from the picnic area, passing the Appalachian Trail. Watch for piled rocks in this grown-over former farmland. Continue down to a switchback at 0.4 mile. Twist and turn three more times before coming to South River, which is a small but wide creek at this point. Cross a side branch and appreciate the lush streamside environment.

SOUTH RIVER FALLS

Yellow birch trees shade mossy rocks and ferns. Violets, toothworts, white trilliums, and wild geraniums color the moist margins, as do straight-trunked tulip trees and gray beeches. Other wildflowers include trout lilies, false Solomon's seals, jack-in-the-pulpits, and columbines. Come to a second tributary at 0.7 mile. The valley narrows, and so does the stream. Cross a rock field at 1.0 mile, and then step across a boulder-filled tributary. Ahead and to your right is the top of the falls, but keep going; there's a better and safer viewpoint a short distance past the granite overhang to your left. Walk out on the outcrop, which is bordered with a man-made stone wall to your right. Gaze upon South River Falls. It spills over a rock face and then splits into two chutes charging downward.

For a different perspective, continue down the trail, reaching a junction at 1.4 miles. Veer right toward the base of the falls. Curve past a tributary into a fertile wildflower zone. Descend to river level again, reaching a flat. Head upriver on a narrow foot trail, passing an impressive fractured rock rampart to your right. Stone steps aid your ascent. Reach the base of South River Falls at 2.1 miles. Looking up, you can clearly see the narrow chute splitting in two before resuming a calmer path toward the sea. This second view adds impressive perspective to the falls.

DIRECTIONS From Harrisonburg, take US 33 west 23 miles to Shenandoah National Park's Swift Run Gap entrance station. Find the trailhead at South River Picnic Area, at milepost 62.8 on Skyline Drive. The picnic area entrance is 2.7 miles north of the entrance station. The path starts at the back of the picnic area on the one-way loop road. The trailhead will be on your right.

GPS TRAILHEAD COORDINATES 38.380217, -78.515650

11 UPPER DOYLES RIVER FALLS, LOWER DOYLES RIVER FALLS, AND JONES RUN FALLS
[7.0-mile loop, strenuous]

This hike visits three major cataracts and numerous other cascades while exploring two boulder-strewn canyons connected by the Appalachian Trail. The hike up Jones Run passes some old-growth tulip trees with impressive girths. If you catch the falls after a rainstorm, you will be well rewarded—falling water is all over the place then. Civil War history enhances the hike. Start at Browns Gap, through which Confederate general Thomas "Stonewall" Jackson passed in early 1862 while outwitting Union forces in the mountains around the Shenandoah Valley. Jackson's local knowledge left the Northerners bamboozled time and again.

Browns Gap was important because of the strategic turnpike that went through it; the turnpike, built in 1805, connected Richmond with the Shenandoah Valley. You will walk the very same turnpike on the first leg of this hike. Think of all the farmers with loads of corn (and liquid corn, also known as moonshine), circuit-riding preachers, traveling hucksters, weary immigrants, and Civil War soldiers who walked this way. And now you're here.

Cross Skyline Drive, descending on Browns Gap Fire Road, the current name of the turnpike. (Madison Run Fire Road, which leaves west from the gap near the parking area, is the western relic of this turnpike.) Look for a small path leaving the road to your left at mile 0.4. Scramble a few feet up this path to the grave of William H. Howard, a Confederate soldier. A carved stone slab

UPPER DOYLES RIVER FALLS

JONES RUN FALLS

marks the location of his interment. Return to the fire road and continue down the trail on a gentle grade.

Cross an iron bridge spanning shallow Doyles River to make a trail junction at 1.7 miles. Turn right onto Doyles River Trail. Other hikers, having come from Skyline Drive and the upper Doyles River Trailhead, will be joining you. The footpath descends along lively Doyles River. Cross the waterway, an easy rock-hop, at mile 1.9.

Doyles River Trail continues along the watercourse but swings away as it approaches Upper Doyles Falls. At 2.1 miles, a side trail leads to the dark pool at the base of the three-tiered, 30-foot waterfall. The cataract spills into a boulder-filled glen at the point where a tributary feeds the river. The canyon tightens; Doyles River continues making frenzied drops. Unnamed cascades accompany you downstream until a sharp switchback leads to the base of Lower Doyles Falls at mile 2.4. At 63 feet, Lower Doyles Falls is the steeper and more spectacular of the two. It dives over a rock lip and then spills in ribbons and channels over multiple tiers. It finally lands in a pool before charging on. The cataract will display different faces depending on the water flow.

Lower Doyles River Falls

    The trail squeezes down the narrow, very rugged gorge, using a wooden bridge to span a tributary spilling into Doyles River at 2.7 miles. At 2.9 miles, find a deep pool between fast-moving rapids. At 3.1 miles, come to a trail marker and the end of Doyles River Trail. Jones Run and Doyles River merge below the signpost. Veer right on lesser-used Jones Run Trail. Begin climbing, and then rock-hop Jones Run at 3.3 miles. Impressive tulip trees grow tall and wide, with such large diameters that it would take several hikers to encircle them.

    Look up the slope. Jones Run gorge is littered with huge boulders. Keep an eye on the creek, too, as many scenic cascades tumble down the relentless watercourse, including some long slide cascades. At 3.8 miles, step over a tributary and then arrive at Jones Run Falls, where water spills 45 feet over a solid rock wall. Large waterside rock slabs make for good observation points. The chilly air and mist from the cataract will cool a hot and sweaty hiker.

    The trail turns sharply left, circumventing a rock rampart. Achieve the top of the falls. The path traces Jones Run past more cascades before veering away from the creek. At 5.0 miles, join an old wagon road. The path widens. Step over Jones Run, diminutive at this point at 5.2 miles. Jones Run Trail ascends and makes a sharp left turn at 5.4 miles. Meet the Appalachian Trail at 5.7 miles. The Jones Run Trailhead and parking area are just steps away. Turn right on the Appalachian Trail, northbound. Dry species such as mountain laurel and chestnut oak straddle the grade back to Browns Gap. Pass spur trails to Dundo Picnic Area at 6.3 miles. Intermittent views of Cedar Mountain open. The Appalachian Trail descends before arriving at Browns Gap at 7.0 miles.

> **DIRECTIONS** From Charlottesville, take I-64 west 23 miles to Shenandoah National Park's Rockfish Gap entrance station. Take Skyline Drive north for 21.6 miles to the trailhead, on your left. The hike starts at the Browns Gap parking area, milepost 83.0 on Skyline Drive.
>
> **GPS TRAILHEAD COORDINATES** 38.240483, -78.710467

12 BIG BRANCH FALLS
[7.6-mile out-and-back, strenuous]

This delicate slide waterfall is most rewardingly accessed from Skyline Drive, thus availing a solitude-filled trek. The vast majority of visitors start from Charlottesville Reservoir, making their way up to the falls. Big Branch Falls can run low by summer, so make your visit from late winter through spring.

Your waterfall hike leaves Blackrock Gap (2,330′) and descends Moormans River Fire Road. The Appalachian Trail is just to your right. At 0.1 mile, step over a small branch that the trail begins to parallel. Pass through pine, black gum, oak, and hickory woodland with an understory of mountain laurel, descending gently on the wide doubletrack. The branch you crossed drops steeply for North Fork Moormans River.

At 1.1 miles, come to a gate on the road; you are leaving the park for a period. The trail stays on a right-of-way, descending to a junction at 1.5 miles. Turn right and immediately cross North Fork Moormans River on rocks. At higher flows this may be a ford. The trail follows the river downstream. Look for ironwood and black birch in this deep vale. Wildflowers color the trailside in spring. At 1.6 miles, a private road splits left; stay right, passing a ramshackle hunter's camp on your left. Look for the smooth gray trunks of the many beech trees that grow in the area; their nuts are a favored food source for wildlife.

Make another rock-hop of the river at 2.0 miles. You will stay on the west bank for the remainder of the hike. Bisect a small grassy clearing. Reenter the park at the crossing of Little Gale Branch at 2.1 miles. The road takes on a more overgrown appearance. Tightly grown, spindly trees are rising from what once was barren soil, remnants of a cataclysmic flood back in the 1990s. We saw this valley then, and the reforestation is truly amazing.

Cross Shop Run at 2.3 miles. The metal remains of an old bridge lie in state here. Before the 1995 flood, Shenandoah National Park maintained this trail as a fire road. Step over an unnamed perennial stream at 2.7 miles. Come back along North Fork Moormans River at 2.9 miles. Tulip trees and sycamores rise from the streamside. Gigantic boulders, gravel bars, speedy shoals, and quiet pools—some deep enough for a dip—all intermingle below. Streamside open rock slabs beckon a visit. Brook trout, rock bass, and smallmouth bass ply the waters.

Come to Big Branch at 3.7 miles. You can see the lower drops of Big Branch Falls from the main trail. Step over the stream and then take the 0.1-mile side trail leading right to the falls. This canyon was gouged back in 1995, exposing the rock bed of the creek, making the entire scene more dramatic. The low-volume cataract drops 30 feet into a plunge pool, and then another cascade slides into a second pool. The third and lowermost drop dips into the deepest pool. As you explore the falls, avoid slick spots on the open rock slabs adjacent to the moving water.

DIRECTIONS From Charlottesville, take I-64 west 23 miles to Shenandoah National Park's Rockfish Gap entrance station. Take Skyline Drive north for 17.7 miles to Black Rock Gap, milepost 87.4. This is where Moormans River Fire Road begins.

GPS TRAILHEAD COORDINATES 38.206850, -78.749683

Waynesboro

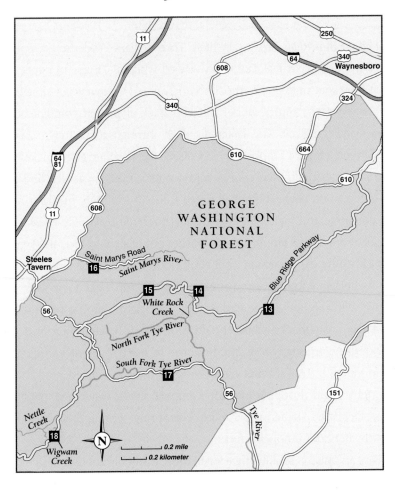

13 FALLS OF CAMPBELL CREEK
[4.2-mile round-trip, moderate]

Located off the Blue Ridge Parkway in busy Three Ridges Wilderness, Upper and Lower Campbell Creek Falls are often viewed while making a 13.1-mile backpacking loop that utilizes the Appalachian Trail (AT). However, a straight shot to the cataracts is a much shorter out-and-back affair that combines the AT and the Mau Tar Trail. The waterfalls dash through rock-strewn Campbell Creek Canyon. Upper Campbell Creek Falls, 20 feet of white glory, makes a slim drop that angles right, then crashes into a mossy boulder garden and finally flows into a pool. Lower Campbell Creek Falls, 30 feet high, bisects a narrow cut in the gorge and makes an angled slide bordered by mossy rocks, ending in a pool. From there Campbell Creek crashes out of sight to meet the Tye River.

Pick up the Appalachian Trail southbound on the east side of the Blue Ridge Parkway at Reeds Gap. Cruise a mown strip next to woods and a meadow, with the Blue Ridge Parkway to your right. Climb a bit at 0.3 mile, using a few switchbacks. Make the crest of Meadow Mountain at 0.6 mile. Gently descend among woods and boulders to reach a gap at 1.4 miles. Here, join the Mau Tar Trail leaving right, avoiding the gated forest road that also leaves right. Begin dropping into the Campbell Creek watershed, passing the Maupin Field trail shelter at 1.5 miles. The spring serving this shelter forms the headwaters of Campbell Creek.

Pass an outsize pool fed by a small drop, easily big enough for a dip, then come to Upper Campbell Creek Falls at 2.0 miles, to the right of the trail. The cataract is near enough the trail to hear, but exercise caution as the angled spiller tumbles through a slot canyon. Lesser cataracts and pools entertain as you continue down Campbell Creek.

To reach Lower Campbell Creek Falls, at 2.1 miles, take the spur trail right to and through a campsite. Keep toward the water and carefully scramble to the base of the spiller. From here, it is easy to see how the convergence of mossy rock forces the water into the tight, boulder-filled slot through which it tumbles.

DIRECTIONS From Exit 96 on I-64 near Waynesboro, take Mount Torry Road/VA 624 south for 1.5 miles, then keep left (south) at Lyndhurst, where

FALLS OF CAMPBELL CREEK

Mount Torry Road changes to VA 664. Stay with VA 664 for 11.3 miles to emerge onto the Blue Ridge Parkway at Reids Gap. The trailhead parking area is on the east side of the Blue Ridge Parkway.

GPS TRAILHEAD COORDINATES 37.902500, -78.985167

14 WHITE ROCK FALLS
[1.8-mile out-and-back, moderate]

The Youth Conservation Corps built White Rock Falls Trail in 1979. Find the singletrack trail across the Parkway and just a little south from The Slacks Overlook. Begin descending a tributary of White Rock Creek in classic hickory–oak woods.

Bridge a creek and then reach an overlook at 0.5 mile. Gaze down into the Tye River Valley. White Rock Falls is below, but stay with the maintained trail along a cliffline, then switchback to reach the spur to White Rock Falls at 0.9 mile. Shortly view the slender spiller frothing into a rock-walled amphitheater complete with a dunking pool. White Rock Falls is a small-volume waterfall, but it spills 30 feet into an incredible gorge. The walls of the narrow canyon embrace you on three sides, and old-growth trees tower above. Although the creek is small, the pool at the base of the falls is big enough to enjoy a swim.

Downstream, White Rock Creek flows into the North Fork of the Tye River. A community named White Rock is located at the convergence of the two creeks. The white rock referred to in the creek and town names is the quartz so prevalent in the area.

DIRECTIONS From Exit 99 on I-64 near Waynesboro, join the Blue Ridge Parkway at milepost 0 and head south to milepost 19.9, Slacks Overlook, on

WHITE ROCK FALLS

the right. To find the trailhead, cross the road and walk north about 60 yards. A sign (look down the slope toward the woods) marks the trail's beginning.

GPS TRAILHEAD COORDINATES 37.908067, -79.051233

15 MINE BANK CREEK CASCADE
[2.8-mile round-trip, moderate]

Mine Bank Creek Cascade is a little-known slide-type waterfall best seen during winter and spring, times of higher water flow. Solitude is all but guaranteed in this parcel of the Saint Mary's Wilderness. Start your hike directly off the Blue Ridge Parkway. Leave the Mine Bank Creek trailhead and soon pass the Bald Mountain Trail intersection. The singletrack Mine Bank Creek Trail dips into its lush namesake valley, thick with rhododendron, where waterfalls, cascades, and cataracts are constant companions, lorded over by massive boulders and rock ramparts. At 0.9 mile, the trail crosses Mine Bank Creek twice in succession, the last one just above an 18-foot tiered cascade. Cut through the heart of the gorge, reaching Mine Bank Creek Cascade, a long 60-foot slide, at 1.4 miles. The Mine Bank Creek Trail continues down a half mile to the St. Mary's River.

MINE BANK CREEK CASCADE

DIRECTIONS From Exit 205 on I-81/I-64, take VA 606 east for 1.5 miles to Steeles Tavern and US 11. Turn left to head north on US 11 for 0.1 mile, then turn right on VA 56 east. Follow VA 56 east for 5.4 miles to the Blue Ridge Parkway. Join the Blue Ridge Parkway northbound and follow it for 4.1 miles to the Mine Bank Trailhead on your left, just before reaching the more easily identifiable Fork Mountain Overlook, which will be on your right.

GPS TRAILHEAD COORDINATES 37.912028, -79.086889

16 SAINT MARY'S WATERFALL
[4.4-mile out-and-back, easy]

Saint Mary's Waterfall is in Saint Mary's Wilderness, which is part of George Washington National Forest. The wilderness tract covers more than 10,000 acres, making it one of the largest wilderness areas in Virginia.

The area's elevation varies from 1,700 to 3,600 feet. The highest point is Cellar Mountain, which has rocky bluffs near the base. You will find that oak and hickory rule the forest. Other vegetation includes sumac, black birch, rhododendron, laurel, and, our favorite, blueberries. Saint Mary's River and its tributaries contain a large population of native trout, and the wildland makes good bear habitat.

Saint Mary's Trail totals 6.2 miles. From the barrier gate, hike along Saint Mary's River on an old roadbed and then a dried-up stream. Numerous floods have caused washouts. After crossing the river (you may have to wade across during high water), you will reach a signed trail intersection. Here, Saint Mary's Trail bears right and heads toward the crest of the Blue Ridge to Green Pond, a 1-acre, high-elevation bog.

But the trail to the falls stays left and passes through a campsite and across Saint Mary's River again to enter Saint Mary's Gorge. After 0.8 mile, Saint Mary's Waterfall spills over a 10-foot ledge between the quartzite walls of this miniature canyon. Jagged boulders and short cliffs surround the large pool at the base.

The historical highlight in Saint Mary's Wilderness is a surface-mining excavation. There is a creek, a waterfall, a trail, and a mountain—all with the name Mine Bank. Pulaski Iron Company mined the valley for iron ore and manganese, running a railroad spur from the Shenandoah Valley up the Saint

Mary's River to its confluence with Chimney Branch. Several mine openings and processing areas sprung up in the Saint Mary's Valley. The mining period started in 1910, ramping up during World War I, then tapered off. By the 1950s, the mining had petered out. Evidence of mining operations remains in the forest. USGS topographic maps show four old mine sites on a section of Saint Mary's Trail beginning less than 1 mile past the waterfall spur. Several trails in this wilderness area follow the former tramline or old mining roads.

Within the boundaries of Saint Mary's Wilderness, there are more than 15 miles of trail, including Mine Bank, Bald Mountain, Cellar Mountain, and Cold Springs Trails. From the parking lot on Saint Mary's Road to 500 feet past the falls, group size is limited to fewer than 10 people, and camping and fires are not allowed within 150 feet of the trail.

DIRECTIONS From Exit 205 on I-81/I-64, take VA 606 east 1.5 miles to Steeles Tavern and US 11. Turn left on US 11 north and follow it 0.1 mile, then turn right on VA 56 east and follow it 1.1 miles to VA 608. Bear left when VA 608 splits off from VA 56, and drive 2.4 miles to a right turn onto Saint Mary's Road. This road becomes gravel within a few hundred yards and ends at a parking area after 1.4 miles. The trailhead is at the upper end beyond the information board.

GPS TRAILHEAD COORDINATES 37.925233, -79.139217

17 CRABTREE FALLS

[3.6-mile out-and-back, moderate]

Crabtree Falls might be the highest waterfall east of the Mississippi, depending on how you qualify a waterfall, but it is doubtless the highest waterfall in Virginia. *Crabtree Falls* is actually a name given to five major waterfalls (and several smaller ones) on Crabtree Creek, which flows into Tye River. Within 0.5 mile, the creek drops 1,200 feet, including one vertical drop of 500 feet. Note that the falls are seasonal. The boldest white drops will be seen from December through May.

Crabtree Falls is a popular attraction, receiving thousands of visitors per year, mostly between May and October. Crabtree Falls is famous for its connection to the classic television show *The Waltons*. The falls were never actually shown, but they were mentioned several times during the life of the program, usually in reference to a Sunday outing.

The name *Crabtree* is thought to have come from William Crabtree, who settled in the area in 1777. Some even say he discovered the waterfall. Another noted pioneer, Allen Tye, while exploring the Blue Ridge, found and named the Tye River for himself.

The land at the base of the falls was almost developed as a resort area in the late 1960s. Landowner Hugh D. Bolton put up NO TRESPASSING signs and stated that he wanted to create a place called Living Waters. The residents of Nelson County encouraged involvement from the U.S. Forest Service (USFS), which had purchased acreage around the falls since the 1930s through small acquisitions and land exchanges, acquiring the falls in 1972. In 1968, after many unsuccessful offers to purchase the land at the base of the falls, legal proceedings began to obtain the two tracts, and the USFS won.

The land became part of the George Washington National Forest, and the waterfall trail has since been developed into a showpiece of the Pedlar Ranger District. There are wooden stairs, gravel paths, and railed overlooks, and many switchbacks ease the climb to the exciting cascades.

The track starts out paved to the first waterfall overlook, then becomes natural surface. The first of many observation decks begins at the end of the paved part of the trail. The path continues 1.7 more miles to the last waterfall overlook, switchbacking ever upward. Then the path follows Crabtree Creek 1.4 miles farther through a sliver of yellow birch, striped maple, and American elm to Crabtree Meadows, an open area with scattered crab apple and apple trees; in the 1930s, several families lived here. The Appalachian Trail can be accessed from Crabtree Meadows via a 0.5-mile side trail.

Be careful at Crabtree Falls. More than 30 deaths and many injuries have occurred since the USFS began keeping records in 1982. Therefore, the USFS maintains a four-wheel-drive road at the top of the falls primarily for use in rescues. Finally, check out the wooden footbridge over the Tye River, now used to connect the lower parking lot to the upper parking lot (The trail used to start at the lower parking lot). There is also a small picnic area here.

DIRECTIONS From Exit 205 on I-81/I-64, take VA 606 east 1.5 miles to Steeles Tavern and US 11. Turn left on US 11 north and follow it 0.1 mile, then turn right on VA 56 east and follow it 12.5 miles to Crabtree Falls Trailhead, across the Tye River. The trail begins at the upper end of the parking lot across the auto bridge over the Tye River. To reach Crabtree Meadows, head back toward the Blue Ridge Parkway for 2.8 miles and turn left onto Forest Road 826. The upper trailhead is 4 miles down and on the left.

GPS TRAILHEAD COORDINATES 37.851002, -79.079854

~~~~~~~~~~~~~~~~~~~~~~~~~~~~~~~~~~~~

18 WIGWAM FALLS

[0.4-mile loop, easy]

~~~~~~~~~~~~~~~~~~~~~~~~~~~~~~~~~~~~

The short hike to 30-foot Wigwam Falls is convenient to the Blue Ridge Parkway. It is worth a visit if you are on the Parkway, especially in spring. To reach Wigwam Falls, follow the easy and short Yankee Horse Trail on the east side of the Parkway through open hardwood forest. The waterfall is actually not on Wigwam Creek but on a small tributary, which can just about dry up in the summer. When the leaves are off the trees, you can see Wigwam Falls from the road.

During your visit, learn about the logging in the area and see the 200-foot reconstructed track of an old railroad. This narrow-gauge line was part of the Irish Creek Railway, built by the South River Lumber Company to access trees that were untouched until the early 1900s. The area was logged out by the late 1930s.

Yankee Horse Trail has a story behind its name. This area was visited by Confederate general Thomas "Stonewall" Jackson's troops during the Civil War. Supposedly, a Union soldier's horse fell here and had to be shot. The nearby Wigwam Mountain is said to be an ancient American Indian hunting ground. This Parkway overlook includes a picnic table and an interpretive sign.

DIRECTIONS From Exit 205 on I-81/I-64, take VA 606 east 1.5 miles to Steeles Tavern and US 11. Turn left on US 11 north and follow it 0.1 mile, then turn right on VA 56 east and follow it 5.4 miles to the Blue Ridge Parkway. From there, head south 7 miles to milepost 34.4, Yankee Horse Ridge Parking Area. The trailhead is marked and obvious.

GPS TRAILHEAD COORDINATES 37.809382, -79.179653

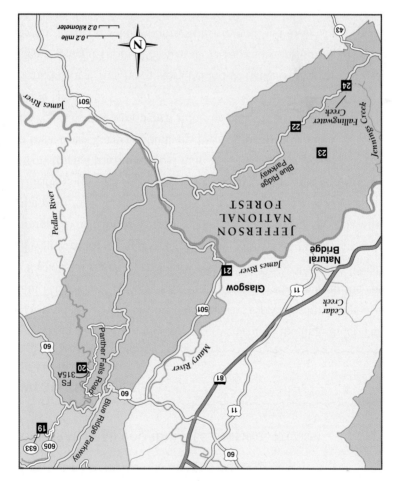

Glasgow

19 STATONS CREEK FALLS
[mileage and difficulty not applicable]

Statons Creek Falls, on Statons Creek, secured its name from a local family; William Staton of Amherst County, an early landowner in the area, may have owned property along the creek. Now the area around the falls is part of the Pedlar Ranger District of George Washington National Forest. Other names for Statons Creek Falls include Lace Falls and Deadman's Falls. The last name is a result of accidents that happen here annually, so always be prudent around falls.

The words of Michael T. Shoemaker perfectly describe Statons Creek Falls: "It is composed of several falls and cascades, which when added together descend a great height. The interesting feature of Statons Creek Falls is not the height, however, but the distinctive zigzag pattern of the series of falls."

The falls descends about 140 feet, and the first drop of 15 feet is across the road from the parking area. This first drop is the only easy part of the falls to access. The farther you go, the more challenging it is to view or photograph this cataract. An 80-foot plunge follows immediately as the creek continues to crash through the gorge. About 1 mile from the falls, Statons Creek flows into Pedlar River.

On Fiddlers Green Way to Statons Creek Falls, about 0.5 mile before you reach the parking area, there is a small pulloff on the left. This is an area of old-growth forest. Logging in the early 1900s bypassed this small stand of trees because of the steep hillsides along Statons Creek. Here you will find red oak, white pine, and tulip trees. Some of the huge trees measure 5 feet around and 100 feet tall.

DIRECTIONS From Exit 188 on I-81 near Buena Vista, head east on US 60 to the Blue Ridge Parkway. Continue east past the Parkway on US 60 for 3.2 miles, where you will see a sign for Oronoco and County Road 605 (Pedlar River Road). Turn left and travel 1.7 miles to a fork. Go right onto County Road 633 (Fiddlers Green Way). The parking area is 1.1 miles up CR 633 on the right.

GPS TRAILHEAD COORDINATES 37.768481, -79.240744

20 PANTHER FALLS

[0.4-mile out-and-back, easy]

Panther Falls is on Pedlar River in the George Washington National Forest. The waterfall's name hearkens back to a time when panthers (often called mountain lions) roamed these parts. It would seem that the river's name recalls a time when peddlers roamed these parts too. However, in his *Hiking Guide to the Pedlar District*, Michael T. Shoemaker notes, "Although peddlers were common along the Pedlar River, the river's name derives from the surname of an early settler who drowned in it." And he continues, "The name of the Pedlar River was in use at least as early as 1742."

Panther Falls is often more a party place than a scenic area; the spot is popular with local college students, though alcohol is not permitted. Pedlar River comes around an S-turn and creates an 8-foot-wide chute where the river squeezes between two huge boulders. This powerful sluice falls 10 feet into a blue-green pool before sliding over a smaller drop.

The swimming hole below the falls is the primary attraction, and people dive off the boulders surrounding the pool. Big sunning rocks are an added attraction. At certain points, the water is more than 20 feet deep, but a sign warns of submerged rocks. Several people have lost their lives here. Strong currents and undertow are of concern to swimmers.

On the drive to Panther Falls, after turning onto Forest Road 315A, you will pass Robert's Creek Cemetery, one of many old family cemeteries in the Pedlar Ranger District. The cemeteries mark homesites from the pioneer days. Rock piles, terraces, and cleared land show evidence of farming from the late 1700s until the Depression.

Begin your hike at the gate. The road here was closed to vehicles long ago. A gradual descent on an old roadbed takes you down to Pedlar River. Signs tacked on trees read TROUT FISHING WATERS. Pedlar River is stocked several times in the spring (and in the fall if the water level cooperates). Follow the river a short distance to the falls.

DIRECTIONS From Exit 188 on I-81 near Buena Vista, head east on US 60 to the Blue Ridge Parkway. Continue east on US 60, just past the Parkway, and turn right onto Panther Falls Road, a well-graded gravel road. Travel 3.4 miles and turn left onto Forest Road 315A, a 0.5-mile side road that ends in a parking circle. The trailhead is beyond the wooden information board at the lower end of the parking lot. The trail begins down the old roadbed past the gate.

GPS TRAILHEAD COORDINATES 37.706310, -79.289756

21 LACE FALLS
[2.0-mile out-and-back, easy]

Lace Falls is located at Natural Bridge State Park, the famous attraction that has been called one of the Seven Wonders of the World. The incredible limestone arch, 215 feet high and 90 feet across, definitely upstages 50-foot Lace Falls. A brochure states that the bridge "once was the summit of a large waterfall. During the 100 million years Cedar Creek flowed, there were also subterranean passageways in the softer stone under the existing arch, which eventually washed away, leaving the harder rock of the structure you see now."

Pick up a map when you arrive, and follow the self-guided tour through this Natural Historic Landmark turned Virginia state park. You will learn about the US president who first owned the Natural Bridge and see another US president's initials carved in the rock. The Monacan Indians believed the bridge, a gift from the Great Spirit, helped their people escape from the Shawnee and Powhatans. According to legend, a canyon interfered with the Monacans' retreat, but after they kneeled in prayer, a bridge appeared across the canyon. The Monacans called it "the Bridge of God."

Start from the gift shop and walk alongside Cascade Creek, with its tumbling waters and small cascades. You will pass a stand of arborvitae, an evergreen in the pine family; the largest trees are 1,000 years old. As the trail turns to the right, descending into the steep ravine formed by Cedar Creek, you get your first view of the Natural Bridge. In addition to this impressive natural wonder, you will pass Cedar Creek Cafe, Cathedral Wall, Monacan Indian Village, Saltpeter Cave, Hemlock Grove, and the spur to the Lost River Site. This is a most impressive nature trail. The trail ends at a circular observation area where you can view Lace Falls flowing over travertine boulders.

The Natural Bridge of Virginia includes several other attractions, such as an underground cavern, a butterfly garden, a historic hotel, a dining room, and a gift shop.

DIRECTIONS From Exit 175 on I-81 between Lexington and Roanoke, take US 11/Lee Highway north a short distance to reach the Natural Bridge. The hike starts at the park visitor center, aka Bridge Entrance & Gift Shop. The state park is open year-round and has an admission fee.

GPS TRAILHEAD COORDINATES   37.628499, -79.543196

22 APPLE ORCHARD FALLS
[2.6-mile out-and-back, easy–moderate]

On the Blue Ridge Parkway stretch of the drive to Apple Orchard Falls, you will travel from the lowest point on the entire Parkway to the highest point on the Parkway in Virginia. The James River (668′) at milepost 63.7 is only 13 miles from milepost 76.7 (3,950′) near Apple Orchard Overlook. The area around Apple Orchard Falls Trail was once owned and logged by the Virginia Lumber and Extract Company. The U.S. Forest Service bought the land in 1917. A ceremony took place in 1987 dedicating the path as a National Recreation Trail.

Apple Orchard Falls flows down the west side of Apple Orchard Mountain (4,225′). The orchard on Apple Orchard Mountain is really an oak woodland, a form of northern hardwood forest that has been dwarfed by the extreme weather at this high elevation. The stunted northern red oaks and the lack of shrubs create an orchard of sorts, and the trees resemble apple trees from a distance.

Apple Orchard Falls Trail begins at Sunset Fields. The grassy clearing and excellent western view attract visitors who want to watch the sun go down. Hike to the falls in the late afternoon, timing your return to catch the sunset over the mountains.

The first part of the Apple Orchard Falls Trail is asphalt and all access, leading across the small roadside meadow. From there, join a singletrack, natural-surface path descending into rich hardwoods. Circle around an upland cove. At 0.2 mile, intersect the Appalachian Trail. Stay straight with the Apple Orchard Falls Trail, as it begins a headlong descent along a fast-gathering, unnamed

APPLE ORCHARD FALLS

tributary of North Creek that makes small cascades while following the rules of gravity. At 0.6 mile, spot some old rock walls from a hardscrabble farm. Life must have been tough up here, with cold winters; thin, sloped soils chock-full of rocks; and extreme isolation. At 0.8 mile, come to Apple Orchard Falls Road, which is closed to vehicles. Keep straight, still descending on the Apple Orchard Falls Trail. Step over a trickling branch contributing its waters to Apple Orchard Falls, then rejoin the main creek, which has now picked up steam and volume as it dashes between boulders. At 1.0 mile, squeeze through a boulder garden, a stone portal of sorts, and then cross the main creek on a hikers' bridge, near a campsite and small ledge waterfall upstream of the bridge.

The valley opens beyond the bridge, and you make a wide switchback. Work down a remarkable number of wooden stairs, heading for Apple Orchard Falls. Pass a big boulder and cleared overlook at 1.2 miles. Here, you can gaze westerly into ridges and hills toward the James River Valley. Continue negotiating wooden steps through rhododendron and mountain laurel. At 1.3 miles, reach a bridge crossing the base of Apple Orchard Falls. The span makes for an ideal viewing platform. Look up—from here you can see the cataract spill over an open ledge and then slide down an angled chute. From there the foam encounters a huge midcataract boulder, where water disperses into multiple spills and then filters into a rock jumble as it passes underneath the bridge. There is a little bit of everything in this waterfall.

DIRECTIONS From Exit 167 on I-81, northeast of Roanoke, take US 11 south 1.2 miles to the town of Buchanan. Turn left on VA 43 east. Follow it 4.7 miles to reach the Blue Ridge Parkway. Turn left and follow the Parkway to Sunset Fields Overlook at milepost 78.4. The trailhead is in the middle of the parking area.

GPS TRAILHEAD COORDINATES 37.507567, -79.523800

23 CORNELIUS CREEK CASCADES
[2.8-mile round-trip, moderate]

Overshadowed by lofty and regal Apple Orchard Falls (see page 64) just one watershed over, Cornelius Creek Cascades is an afterthought for most waterfall lovers in this swath of the Blue Ridge. Admittedly, Cornelius Creek may be a mere 10 feet high, but the frothy spiller presents a fine plunge pool and solitude aplenty. Don't be surprised if the Forest Road 59 trailhead is busy; almost all other hikers will be heading for Apple Orchard Falls (going to those falls from the bottom up, rather than from the Blue Ridge Parkway down). Make sure to join the

CORNELIUS CREEK CASCADES

Cornelius Creek Trail, leading south from the trailhead, rather than the Apple Orchard Falls Trail, heading up east North Creek.

The Cornelius Creek valley starts out wide, and the trail takes you through flats away from the stream. At 0.8 mile, rock-hop over to the left-hand bank of Cornelius Creek. Here, the valley narrows. The scenic, moderate hike continues up dashing Cornelius Creek, displaying additional shoals with crystalline pools.

At 1.2 miles, a bridge leads over Cornelius Creek just above a 10-foot slide cascade dancing over weathered rock. The span gives you a dry-footed, top-down view of this sloped spiller. Rock-hop to the left-hand bank at 1.3 miles. You can't miss trailside Cornelius Creek Cascades at 1.4 miles, with its classic inverted fan-shaped, 10-foot drop over a mossy stone rampart into a wide plunge pool replete with hearty trout. The cataract makes for a chilly but refreshing summertime swimming hole.

DIRECTIONS From Exit 168 (Arcadia) on I-81 near Buchanan, take VA 614 east 3.2 miles, then turn left on North Creek Road/FR 59. Follow North Creek Road 2.8 miles, passing North Creek Campground, then continue straight as the road becomes gravel. Drive 1.7 more miles to dead-end at the trailhead.

GPS TRAILHEAD COORDINATES 37.529806, -79.553194

24 FALLINGWATER CASCADES
[1.5-mile loop, moderate]

This hike delivers looks at Fallingwater Cascades from multiple vantages: from below at a distance; from its base, beside the cataract; and from above it. These different viewpoints deliver an added appreciation of the 100-plus-foot, sloping, slipping spiller and allow you to see the entirety of Fallingwater Cascades.

The 1.6-mile loop down to Fallingwater Cascades is pretty easy—doable by children and older hikers—though parts of the pathway are boulder-strewn and irregular. Leave Wilkinson Gap and the Flat Top parking area on the Fallingwater Cascades Trail, a designated National Recreation Trail built in 1982. Walk down from the west side of the Blue Ridge Parkway on a singletrack, natural-surface path. Immediately enter an impressive grove of old-growth tulip trees. These towering giants somehow escaped the logger's ax. Quickly reach the loop portion of the hike. Keep straight here, drifting into the steep-sided Fallingwater Creek valley. This stream is born on the slopes of Chestnut Mountain and Floyd Mountain, cutting a chasm to meet its mother stream, Jennings Creek, which then flows on to feed the James River. Pines and rocks border the path.

At 0.5 mile, come to Fallingwater Creek and a contemplation bench. There has been a bridge here in the past, and there may be one in the future, but be prepared to rock-hop the watercourse. Here is the Catch-22 of waterfall hiking: If the falls are vigorous, then crossing the stream might be challenging. If such is the case, you'll need to take off your shoes and make a short wade. However, if the stream is low, the crossing will be an easy rock hop, but the falls will be less bold. Just hope the bridge has been rebuilt when you come here. Periodic floods have repeatedly washed it out in the past.

In the gorge depths, huge boulders and rock walls are interspersed with moving water. Vegetation finds its place where soil and slope allow. Ascend along Fallingwater Creek after crossing it, passing lesser cascades. The terrain is rugged and steep, and the canyon hems you in. Stone steps, wood steps, and rock walls aid your passage through this decidedly non-trail-friendly terrain. At 0.6 mile, reach an intersection. Keep straight, soon finding the base of 100-foot Fallingwater Cascades. The cataract spills over a naked rock face into a shallow pool at your feet. The lowermost part of the waterfall is visible from here, but the uppermost fall is too sloped to view in its entirety. The open rock face forms a light gap, even when summer's growth is its thickest. Boulders to sit on and photo perches enhance the setting.

Backtrack to continue the loop, climbing to another spur path that leads to the top of the falls, skirting a stone wall. Use caution here, as slippery stone slabs are numerous. The open rock face of the falls allows you to look downstream beyond the spreading valley toward the Peaks of Otter.

Continue up the geologically fascinating vale. Look back in this area at a host of mountains through the window formed by the valley of Fallingwater Creek. The sharp top of Sharp Top is easily discernible. Harkening Hill is visible too. The wild terrain makes civilization seem far away. Bridge Fallingwater Creek at 0.8 mile. Rock slabs below the wooden footbridge make for ideal relaxation spots.

The trail then aims for the parkway in pine–oak–mountain laurel woods. Pass the Fallingwater Overlook and alternate parkway parking at 1.2 miles. Continue uphill in woods, drifting over a knob to finish the loop. From there, turn left, reaching Wilkinson Gap and the Flat Top parking area at 1.5 miles.

The Peaks of Otter recreation area features not only this trek but also other hikes, such as the 1.5-mile trip to Sharp Top, the peak of which can almost be reached by bus, with but 0.3 mile to the top, where 360-degree views await. In addition, Peaks of Otter has a lodge, campground, and picnic area, open in season. You can also visit the Johnson Farm, a restored homestead dating back to 1852, and participate in seasonal live demonstrations at the mountain enclave.

DIRECTIONS From Exit 167 on I-81, about 25 miles northeast of Roanoke, take US 11 south 1.2 miles to the town of Buchanan. Turn left on VA 43 east. Follow it to reach the Blue Ridge Parkway after 4.7 miles. Turn left and follow the Parkway northeast 7.5 miles to milepost 83.5, Flat Top Overlook, on your left, about 2.4 miles beyond the Peaks of Otter Visitor Center. The Fallingwater Cascades Trail starts across from the viewless Flat Top Overlook on the Parkway, opposite the road from the Flat Top Trail, which also starts at this overlook.

GPS TRAILHEAD COORDINATES 37.472900, -79.580350

Fallingwater Cascades

Alleghany Highlands

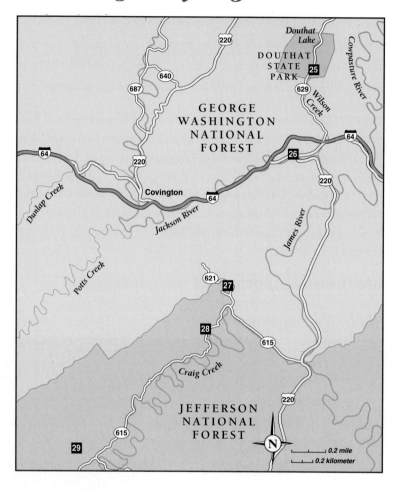

25 STONY RUN FALLS AND BLUE SUCK FALLS
[8.8-mile loop, moderate]

Stony Run Falls and Blue Suck Falls are located in Douthat State Park, established in 1936 as one of the first six state parks in Virginia. The Civilian Conservation Corps (CCC) left its mark with fine Depression-era landscaping, stone masonry, and wood craftsmanship throughout the park. While the waterfalls won't knock your socks off, the state park as a whole—recognized as a National Historic District—is very impressive.

Douthat lies between two mountain ridges in the Alleghany Highlands and covers close to 4,500 acres. Wilson Creek runs through the park, north to south, paralleling VA 629. A dam, built by the CCC, impounds the 50-acre Douthat Lake, and the list of facilities is long: a store, an amphitheater, a restaurant, a campground, 30 cabins, two lodges, a boat ramp, and boat and bike rentals. You can lunch under one of three picnic shelters, swim at designated beaches, fish from the creek or the lake, mountain bike, and, of course, hike.

Douthat State Park offers more than 40 miles of hiking trails. This waterfall loop consists of four trails: Stony Run, Tuscarora Overlook, Blue Suck Falls, and Tobacco House Ridge Trails.

Beginning at the trailhead for Stony Run, you will climb gradually, gaining 300 feet in elevation, to Stony Run Falls. At a sharp switchback, mile 1.7, follow the short side trail to the falls. The ascent continues as you scale Middle Mountain on several switchbacks. Once on Tuscarora Overlook Trail, come to a grassy clearing and a restored CCC fire-watch cabin. This maintained overlook affords the most beautiful view in the park. Look west down into the basin of Wilson Creek and across toward the distant Beards Mountain on the park's east boundary. Blue Suck Falls Trail leads you to another superb view from Lookout Rock (2,560´), and then descends on switchbacks through a hollow along Blue Suck Run to cross the base of Blue Suck Falls at 7.5 miles. Do not miss the right turn onto Tobacco House Ridge Trail, which takes you to White Oak Campground, Loop C. From there it is a 0.5-mile road walk on County Road 629 back to your vehicle.

Note: The loop trail crosses Stony Run and Blue Suck Run several times, with no bridges, so wear appropriate shoes. Many other trails intersect the loop; watch the colored blazes carefully. Maps are available online and at the park office.

Both Stony Run Falls and Blue Suck Falls are located on runs of the same names. They originate on Middle Mountain, the highest peak in the park. Stony Run and Blue Suck Run flow into Wilson Creek below Douthat Lake. The narrow waterfalls both drop about 50 feet, but Blue Suck Falls has three distinct cascades. Try to visit these creeks after a good rain (usually winter through spring). Later in the year these cataracts can practically run dry.

DIRECTIONS From Exit 27 on I-64, head north on County Road 629 (Douthat Road), which runs through the park. The parking area for Stony Run Falls is 6.5 miles down CR 629 on the left. The park office is on the right after 7 miles.

GPS TRAILHEAD COORDINATES   37.887900, -79.803983

26 FALLING SPRING FALLS
[mileage and difficulty not applicable]

"The only remarkable Cascade in this country, is that of the Falling Spring in Augusta. . . . It falls over a rock 200 feet into the valley below." So wrote Thomas Jefferson in his 1778 *Notes on Virginia.* A trip to Falling Spring Falls is hard to resist after such an extraordinary endorsement from a famous visitor.

Falling Spring Falls is located about 1 hour west of Lexington. Since the land was donated to the state of Virginia in 2004, the vista point accesses have been improved. The view is excellent. The creek dives off the bluff—almost leaping just as the sign in the parking area describes. The first free fall is about 70 feet, and then the creek cascades for another 100 feet or so. From the overlook, you can watch the creek disappear into the valley of Falling Spring.

Falling Spring Falls originates on 60 acres that once made up the world's largest watercress farm. The spring is fed from several underground springs— warm and cold—in separate caves. The combination creates a stream temperature that averages 65.6°F.

Across the road from the waterfall, a bronze plaque affixed to a boulder honors an American Indian fighter and courier who saved Fort Lee from the

OPPOSITE: FALLING SPRING FALLS

photo: *Bill Sharpton*

Indians in the late 1700s. The gunpowder ran out, and the only chance for protecting the fort was a perilous journey to resupply at Camp Union, a 240-mile round-trip that would take three days of travel past enemy forces and through fierce wilderness.

The hero who volunteered when no one else would take the ride was actually a heroine, Ann Bailey, also known as Mad Ann. Her famed horse was a black pony called Liverpool. The plaque was a project of the local chapter of the Daughters of the American Revolution.

DIRECTIONS From Exit 16 on I-64 in Covington, take US 220 North/ US 60 West. (Don't turn right onto County Road 687 for the town of Falling Spring.) After 9.4 miles, look for the sign and parking area indicating the falls on your left.

GPS TRAILHEAD COORDINATES 37.867563, -79.947158

27 ROARING RUN FALLS
[2.0-mile loop, easy-moderate]

After seeing the number of noisy cataracts along Roaring Run, you will agree that the crashing stream is aptly named. It truly does roar where it dives through a gorge, creating falls aplenty. Back in the 1830s, John Garth and Benjamin Scruggs saw the energy potential of Roaring Run and purchased a 9,000-acre tract on which to build an iron ore furnace. These iron furnaces, essentially giant ovens made of stone, needed five things: stone to build the furnace; iron ore and limestone to make the final product; rich forests to make charcoal to fire the furnace; and water to power the giant bellows used to raise temperatures inside the furnace to a point where iron could be made.

The valley of Roaring Run had all five. First, the furnace was built from cut stone quarried a mile distant. Then a water diversion was dug from Roaring Run to power a water wheel that in turn powered the giant bellows. Forests grew rich and magnificent in the Roaring Run valley. The Roaring Run Iron Works was incorporated, and the 36-foot-high furnace was built.

By 1839, the furnace was operating, and over the next three decades furnace tenders melted iron, allowing it to flow into molds. These molds were known as pigs, which is how the name pig iron came to be.

Roaring Run Furnace went through several owners and was rebuilt in 1847 along the way. However, by 1855, the furnace cooled for the final time and most equipment was sold at auction.

Eventually, the property fell into the hands of the U.S. Forest Service. They turned it into a recreation area. Today we have a picnic area, swimming holes, and a trail system that complements the natural beauty of Roaring Run.

The family-friendly 2-mile loop hike cruises past the iron furnace. Look for unnatural mounds of soil, test pits from the ore-searching days. After a half mile you open to a view above the Roaring Run gorge. Shoemaker Knob rises across the chasm, as do the Rye Patch Mountains. Later, come along Roaring Run. Lesser falls are already putting on a show as you climb past them. A 35-foot slide cascade dropping in four stages provides a warm-up.

Pass another fall with a huge swimming hole. Reach Roaring Run Falls a mile from the trailhead. Here, the cataract drops 30 feet over a vegetated rock face. Wide stone slabs border the cataract. It is truly a beauty spot. From the falls, descend through the heart of the Roaring Run gorge. Rock walls, boulders, and crashing water meld with forest, creating memorable scenes.

DIRECTIONS From Exit 150A (if northbound) or Exit 150B (if southbound) on I-81, take US 220 north 8 miles to Fincastle and continue on US 220 for 12 more miles to VA 615/Craig Creek Road, near Eagle Rock. Turn left on VA 615 and follow it 5.5 miles to turn right on Roaring Run Road/VA 621. Follow Roaring Run Road 0.9 mile, then turn left into the Roaring Run Recreation Area, following it 0.3 mile to dead-end at the trailhead.

GPS TRAILHEAD COORDINATES 37.707567, -79.892733

28 HIPES BRANCH CASCADE

[2.2-mile round-trip, easy]

This waterfall adventure uses the Lower Hoop Hole Trail to reach a gorge cutting through the heights of Bald Knob in the Rich Patch Mountains. Here, Hipes Branch slices a canyon rife with exposed craggy cliffs and a sea of boulders, rocks, and pebbles, contrasting in their stillness with Hipes Branch Cascade as it froths into an outsize plunge pool.

Though you can make a 2.2-mile out-and-back hike to Hipes Branch Cascade, I recommend making a 3.3-mile loop heading up Hipes Branch then down the Stony Run gorge—though the Stony Run traverse requires 11 bridge-less stream crossings. However, under normal flows they will all be simple rock hops you can do dry-footed.

To execute the 2.2-mile out-and-back to Hipes Branch Cascade, leave the Hoop Hole parking area, passing an informative trail kiosk. Drop to quickly reach Stony Run, gently coursing over rock beds that belie the stream's alto-gether different nature upstream. Just after the crossing, reach the loop portion of the Lower Hoop Hole Trail. Head left here in former farmland, now grown over in pines, oaks, and galax on a sometimes sandy trailbed.

At 0.7 mile, enter the canyon of Hipes Branch, its pale outcroppings tat-tooed in lichens and moss contrasting with the emerald rhododendron flanking the mountain stream. The size of the pools in relation to the size of the creek will surprise you. At 1.0 mile, make a pair of creek crossings. You are on the right-hand bank of Hipes Branch, heading upstream. At 1.1 miles, a short, rough trail leads left to the outsize plunge pool, at the head of which spills 10-foot Hipes Branch Cascade, making an upper drop over mossy rock, then a second drop into the chilly pool.

At this point you can backtrack to the trailhead. Ambitious hikers will continue up the Lower Hoop Hole Loop, passing a pair of intersections with the Upper Hoop Hole Loop, then turning right down geologically and aquatically intriguing Stony Run Canyon, returning to the trailhead at 3.3 miles.

DIRECTIONS From Exit 150A (if northbound) or Exit 150B (if southbound) on I-81, take US 220 north 8 miles to Fincastle and continue on US 220 for 12 more miles to VA 615/Craig Creek Road, near Eagle Rock. Turn left on VA 615 and follow it 8 miles to turn right into the Hoop Hole trailhead. (*Note:* You will pass the signed right turn toward Roaring Run Recreation Area 2.5 miles before reaching the Hoop Hole trailhead.)

GPS TRAILHEAD COORDINATES 37.673111, -79.917583

29 FENWICK MINES CASCADE
[1.8-mile round-trip, easy]

In the late 1800s, iron ore was discovered around Mill Creek, a tributary of Craig Creek, deep in the Virginia Appalachians. And by 1890, the Low Moor Iron Company established an iron ore mine and a town named Fenwick. *Fen* is another word for "wetland" and the stretch of Mill Creek where the mine and community were located is a wetland to this day. Back then, Fenwick boasted more than 300 residents.

The land is now owned by the U.S. Forest Service and is a day-use recreation area where we can view the 15-foot stairstep cascade on Mill Creek, the former mining community, and the wildlife-rich wetlands on the easy, all-access Wetlands Trail.

Leave the trailhead, then cross Mill Creek on a footbridge. Ahead, stroll on a boardwalk over wetlands before passing a short spur looping a fishing pond. Here, the path comes near VA 685, where you wind through a picnic area and reach an alternate access off VA 685. Here, stay straight, joining the quarter-mile Nature Trail, soon bridging Mill Creek. The Nature Trail ends at an observation deck overlooking the waterfall on Mill Creek. The spiller tumbles about 15 feet over stairstep ledges into a surprisingly large and deep pool bordered by a stone amphitheater, parts of which overhang the stream below. A gravel bar borders the waterfall pool. User-created trails lead to both the top and bottom of the cataract.

DIRECTIONS From Exit 141 on I-81 just south of Roanoke, take VA 419 north 0.3 mile, then turn right on VA 311 north and follow it 19 miles to New Castle. From the intersection of VA 311, VA 42, and VA 615 in downtown New Castle, take VA 615/Craigs Creek Road 5.1 miles to a four-way intersection. Turn left on Peaceful Valley Road/VA 611 and follow it 0.1 mile to turn right on VA 685. Follow VA 685 for 1.6 miles and turn right into the signed Fenwick Mines Recreation Area parking.

GPS TRAILHEAD COORDINATES 37.574222, -80.055500

Southwest Virginia

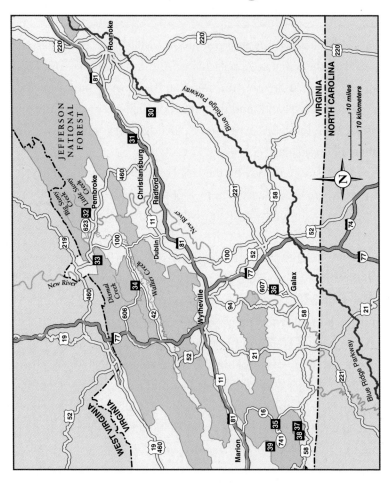

30 BENT MOUNTAIN FALLS
[4.6-mile round-trip, moderate]

Bottom Creek Gorge Preserve, owned and maintained by the Nature Conservancy, is home to Bent Mountain Falls, Virginia's second-tallest waterfall, at 200 feet in height. It is very difficult to reach but is easily viewed from a distance at an overlook. Hikers can make a rewarding loop to this perch, where they can admire Camp Creek making its plunge into Bottom Creek Gorge.

Bottom Creek Gorge Preserve also harbors rare fish and plants as well as homesites, graveyards, and other evidence of families that called the area home, adding human and natural history to this waterfall quest among the 5 miles of trails coursing through the preserve. A basic counterclockwise loop leads you past historic homesites, then to Bent Mountain Falls and onward to a series of pools and rapids on Bottom Creek known as The Kettles before returning to the trailhead. *Note:* Dogs are not allowed in the preserve.

A doubletrack path from the trailhead quickly leads past homesites while rising to an informative trailside kiosk at 0.5 mile. Descend beyond diminishing fields to pass the Knight Trail, your return route, at 0.6 mile. For now, keep straight on the fence-bordered track. Folks settled here in the late 1700s and resided here into the 1950s. Today, these upland fields are reverting to woods, but the Bottom Creek Gorge was always wild, known as The Roughs.

At 0.9 mile, leave right on the Duval Trail. At 1.4 miles, look right for a short spur leading to the small, fence-bordered Hall Cemetery. Only the grave of Emily Hall has an engraved memorial. The others are simply flat fieldstones. Ahead, the trail turns into the Bottom Creek Gorge, passing sloped terrain with pioneer rock piles. At 2.2 miles, split right at a trail intersection, heading toward Bent Mountain Falls overlook, reached at 2.3 miles. Here, peer across the gorge as Camp Creek tumbles into the Bottom Creek chasm, angling down a cliff. It is hard to capture the falls in their entirety, but the sight is worthy nonetheless.

Backtrack from the overlook spur, then take the Johnston Trail uphill. At 2.6 miles, turn right on the Knight Trail, dropping into the gorge to find a water-access spur at 3.0 miles. Here, follow a short path to reach The Kettles, a series of shoals and pools.

Return to the Knight Trail, keeping up the gorge. The Knight Trail ends at 4.0 miles. From here, it is a 0.6-mile backtrack to the trailhead.

DIRECTIONS From the intersection of US 221 and VA 419 in Cave Spring near Roanoke, take US 221 south for 14 miles to County Line Road/VA 644, 0.5 mile after passing a signed left turn toward the Blue Ridge Parkway. Turn right on County Line Road and follow it 1.1 miles to bear right onto VA 669/Bottom Creek Road at the Floyd–Roanoke county line. Stay on VA 669 for 0.9 mile. Here, Bottom Creek Road turns right, but you stay straight on VA 669, which becomes Patterson Drive. Follow Patterson Drive 1.8 miles to bridge Bottom Creek. Just after this bridge turn left into the signed entrance to Bottom Creek Gorge Preserve. Reach a gate at 0.1 mile. Parking is limited here, so please be considerate.

GPS TRAILHEAD COORDINATES   37.133056, -80.182806

BENT MOUNTAIN FALLS   *photo: Sharon McCarthy*

31 FALLS OF FALLS RIDGE PRESERVE

[0.9-mile balloon, easy]

These falls are the most peculiar cascades in the Old Dominion. It is in Falls Hollow where one of the world's largest deposits of exposed calcium carbonate lies. Here, minerals and lime dissolve as the stream of Falls Hollow flows downward, creating strange and otherworldly calcium carbonate deposits, recalling melted rock or a strange combination of soil and stone. Over time these calcium carbonate deposits, commonly known as travertine, have built up, steepening the gradient of the stream within Falls Hollow and creating the rounded stairstep waterfalls that attract so many visitors.

In earlier days, Falls Hollow was owned by the Dudley clan, who farmed, cut timber, raised dairy cattle, and at one time operated a general store and post office. In the 1930s, Harry Dudley saw there was money to be made in the calcium carbonate deposits, by turning them into lime to sell. Mr. Dudley built a concrete kiln to use heat to convert the calcium deposits into lime. This kiln still stands today, and you can see it on this walk. Later, photographer William P. Bradley realized the important natural features of Falls Hollow and bought it. Bradley lived here in retirement, then in 1974 deeded over the 655-acre property to the Nature Conservancy, which established Falls Ridge Preserve.

Visitors access the peculiar cataracts by joining a grassy track southbound through a linear meadow. Leave the meadow at 0.2 mile and reach a trail junction. Head right on the Bradley Trail. Ascend a bit, then reach the main falls of the preserve on a short spur trail left. Here, the stream spills 30 feet over a tan travertine ledge into a shallow, rock-dotted pool, collects, then pushes downstream in small rapids. Depending on the flow, the water will be falling over different parts of the ledge at different rates. Upon closer inspection, you see the odd look and texture of the rock over which the falls spill.

The falls are the most uncommon cascades in the Old Dominion. Lucky are those who see Falls Hollow in a deep freeze, as icicles enhance the already odd characteristics of the cataracts. Continue on the Bradley Trail, circling around the lowermost fall, then bridging the stream at yet another fall. This cataract is much lower but has a much deeper pool. Pass more small but strange waterfalls thinly flowing over travertine slabs. At 0.4 mile, turn away from the stream and the end of the cataracts to make a miniloop. Turn into a lesser hollow, passing smaller caves.

At 0.5 mile, split left, passing near the lime kiln. When this was operating, pieces of the calcium carbonate were blasted from the stream area, loaded onto carts, then pulled by mule to the top of the kiln, where the minerals were processed. The miniloop ends as you return to the water, bridging the stream of Falls Hollow. From there it is a 0.2-mile backtrack to the trailhead, during which you'll be contemplating the atypical waterfalls of this preserve.

DIRECTIONS From Exit 128 (Ironto) on I-81 southwest of Roanoke, follow North Fork Road/VA 603 south 7.0 miles to Falls Ridge Road and the community of Fagg. Turn left onto Falls Ridge Road. Cross a narrow bridge over North Fork Roanoke River to then cross railroad tracks just ahead. Turn left on a dirt road immediately after crossing the railroad track. Follow the dirt road 0.2 mile, then split left at the sign for Falls Ridge Preserve to end at a parking area.

GPS TRAILHEAD COORDINATES 37.193111, -80.321417

FALLS OF FALLS RIDGE PRESERVE

32 CASCADE FALLS
[4.0-mile loop, moderate]

A network of interconnected trails leads up to Cascade Falls. It is a net 700-foot ascent from the trailhead. The trails range from challenging, narrow, and undulating to a well-graded, wide track that makes for the easiest route. No matter which way you go, it is 2 miles by foot to the waterfall. I recommend taking the scenic and exciting Lower Trail first. Carved stone signs located at trail intersections keep you on track. Using stone steps and rock walkways integrated into the incredible landscape, the waterside trails literally get into the heart of the Little Stony Creek valley. And there are boulder gardens, cliffs, cataracts, and an everywhere-you-look beauty that cannot be denied. Be forewarned: Cascade Recreation Area can be very crowded on nice-weather weekends. Solitude seekers should plan their visits for off times.

Begin the hike near the recreation area restrooms. Pass a kiosk and enter woods, quickly meeting up with another path coming from the picnic area. The wide, heavily used trail reaches an intersection at 0.2 mile. Head right on the Lower Trail, crossing Little Stony Creek on Bridge 1. Begin coursing your way up the incredible gorge of Little Stony Creek. The path is fascinating when you consider the extensive construction that went into working it up the rock-walled, boulder-strewn canyon. Stone steps and inlaid stone walkways achieve passage beyond still, deep pools and fast-moving cataracts, past fern clusters and rhododendron thickets. Little Stony Creek is shaded by black birch, yellow birch, and buckeye. The wildflowers can be grand in spring.

At 0.5 mile, view the trailside metal boiler, used to provide steam power for a mobile sawmill that once operated in the valley.

At 1.1 miles, come to Bridge 2. Here, the Lower Trail crosses over to the left-hand bank of Little Stony Creek. A shortcut leads left to the Upper Trail, but stay right and continue up the gorge. Bridges span sheer sides of the canyon, while stone walls, walkways, and other means squeeze you past otherwise impassable terrain. The trail work here is amazing in its own right, yet it doesn't exceed the God-created mosaic of variegated rock, moving water, and diverse vegetation, all enhanced by sunlight piercing the gorge.

CASCADE FALLS

At 1.6 miles, an incoming tributary across the creek creates its own 40-foot cataract while adding its flow to Little Stony Creek. At 1.8 miles, another shortcut leads left to the Upper Trail, but stay on the Lower Trail—you're almost to the star attraction.

Cascade Falls, at 2.0 miles, creates quite a setting. Here, the 60-foot cataract pours over a stone cliff into a huge pool framed by rock walls, ledges, and overhung rock houses. Multiple viewing platforms allow different vantage points, and a dead-end trail cruises near the top of the falls. In summer, visitors will be playing around the fall's base and swimming in the enormous pool below the cataract, in addition to hanging out on nearby rock slabs. I have had the privilege of seeing Cascade Falls at high water and can tell you the roar, the spray, and the raw power are amazing.

After exploring the falls and viewing them from multiple vantage points, take the Upper Trail away from the falls. Climb the side of the gorge to reach a wide track and a trail intersection. Here, at 2.2 miles, the Conservancy Trail leads right, up toward Barneys Wall, but your hike heads left to join the doubletrack Upper Trail. This is essentially a rescue road used by medical personnel to rapidly reach injured visitors at Cascade Falls; mix thousands of annual visitors and a big waterfall and you end up with occasional accidents.

Hikers will appreciate the wide, easy nature of the road after the serpentine, irregular Lower Trail. Moreover, it is downhill just about the whole way. Ahead, pass the uppermost shortcut. Watch for a conspicuous overhanging bluff at 2.5 miles. Reach the shortcut to Bridge 2 at 2.9 miles. Continue downhill in a widening valley. Pass Bridge 1 at 3.8 miles. You have completed the loop. Backtrack 0.2 mile to finish the hike.

DIRECTIONS From Exit 118 on I-81 near Christiansburg, take US 460 west. Drive approximately 26.5 miles to the town of Pembroke. Turn right on Cascade Drive/VA 623. Take Cascade Drive 3.3 miles to dead-end at the trailhead.

GPS TRAILHEAD COORDINATES 37.353502, -80.599549

33 FALLS OF MILL CREEK NATURE PARK
[2.8-mile round-trip, moderate]

Mill Creek Nature Park in Narrows, Virginia, near the New River, is the setting for this waterfall outing along Mill Creek and tributary Mercy Branch, where three spillers await your arrival. Starting the right trail is key to your adventure. Leave the parking area on the Wheezer Trail, and pass near the picnic shelter in a small field. Enter woods and join a wide track, with Mill Creek flowing to your right. Do not take the bridged trail crossing over Mill Creek; it links to the Upper Loop and Lower Loop trails. Don't take the gravel road leading uphill to a water tank, either.

Mill Creek tumbles clear among boulders and rocks, and buckeye, black birch, maple, and other hardwood trees shade the gorge. At 0.4 mile, a short spur leads right to a three-sided wooden trail shelter and picnic area in a small flat. Continue uptrail to reach another intersection. Here, the Wheezer Trail goes left,

FALLS OF MILL CREEK NATURE PARK

but you stay right, joining the Waterfalls Trail. Enter the Jefferson National Forest. Ascend a rocky defile with bluffs rising above. Bisect boulder fields. Mill Creek dances below through a sea of rhododendron. At 1.0 mile, stay right, joining the Catwalk Trail. Shortly come to Mercy Branch at 1.1 miles. Here, Mercy Branch tumbles in cascades both above and below the stream crossing, bringing you bonus falls. Just ahead, reach the first signed spur to a waterfall. Turn right and descend to Mill Creek. Open onto a rock slab in a stone cathedral. Upstream, Mill Creek splashes white 15 feet over a dark layered ledge, flows beside the slab upon which you stand, and then tumbles 10 feet more below the slab into a pool.

Resume the steepening Catwalk Trail. Come to another signed spur trail at 1.3 miles. This longer spur takes you through rhododendron to the lower end of a long, angled cataract starting 80 or more feet above you. There, the narrow spiller dashes in stages, then caroms through a massive boulder garden and continues a little below your viewing spot to slow in stony shoals. This waterfall is more difficult to photograph.

DIRECTIONS From Blacksburg, take US 460 west about 25 miles to the town of Narrows, exiting US 460 at Fleshman Street. Follow Fleshman Street a short distance to turn left onto VA 61 and bridge the New River.

After 0.5 mile on VA 61, turn left on VA 100 south in downtown Narrows. Follow VA 100 south 0.4 mile, then turn right on Northview Street. Follow Northview Street past houses for 1.2 miles to dead-end at Mill Creek Nature Park. Parking is on the left.

GPS TRAILHEAD COORDINATES 37.316944, -80.793778

34 FALLS OF DISMAL
[0.2-mile out-and-back, easy]

What a name! What a waterfall! The Falls of Dismal may not be the highest, the most voluminous, or the widest waterfall in this guide, but it certainly has the most intriguing name. And with a short 0.1-mile path to the falls, almost everyone can enjoy it. If you wish to make it more of a hike, you can join the Appalachian Trail northbound from VA 606. Via that path, it is about 1.4 miles one-way to the Falls of Dismal.

The name of the falls comes from its mother stream, Dismal Creek. It is hard to imagine why such a beautiful Virginia mountain brook was given that moniker; it may have originated from the poor farming in the valley. However,

FALLS OF DISMAL

the falls, scenery, and stream are anything but dismal. The falls themselves are more broad than tall, extending about 50 feet in width. The drop is about 10 feet into a plunge pool bordered by wide stone terraces that make for ideal viewing or repose spots. The left side of the falls drops in stairstep cascades, while the middle and right sides make a curtain–type descent. The plunge pool draws in swimmers. A small, primitive campground, Walnut Flats, is located just a short distance up the forest access road.

DIRECTIONS From Exit 98 on I-81 near Dublin, drive north on VA 100 for 12 miles to VA 42. Turn left and take VA 42 west for 13 miles to VA 606/Wilderness Road. Turn right on VA 606 and follow it 0.9 mile to Dismal Creek Road/VA 671. After 0.4 mile, VA 671 turns to gravel. Drive another 0.5 mile to reach the parking area on your right.

GPS TRAILHEAD COORDINATES 37.187833, -80.900817

35 COMERS CREEK FALLS
[1.2-mile out-and-back, easy]

Comers Creek Falls is well visited due to its great location along the Appalachian Trail (AT). Virginia has the most AT miles of any state—540, give or take. Comers Creek Falls is in southwest Virginia, within Mount Rogers National Recreation Area. The Comers Creek Falls Trail leaves the Smyth–Grayson county line and drops down into the steep valley of Comers Creek past the Iron Mountain Trail (the recreation area's other long-distance hiking trail) to intersect the AT. To access the actual falls, hikers must continue on the AT for 0.1 mile.

Leave VA 741 on the Comers Creek Falls Trail. Walk downstream along Comers Creek, and bridge a wet area on elevated planks. A field lies off to your left. At 0.1 mile, reach the Iron Mountain Trail. Keep straight on the Comers Creek Falls Trail, passing a campsite on your right. Ahead, Comers Creek drops steeply below the path in several small cascades and falls into a rhododendron-choked gorge.

The Comers Creek Falls Trail descends rapidly along with the stream, curving north to intersect the AT at 0.4 mile. To access Comers Creek Falls, turn right on the AT and continue another 0.1 mile to view the cataract. This spiller

COMERS CREEK FALLS

drops about 15 feet in a stairstep fashion. In the summer, sweaty AT hikers will be cooling off in the small plunge pool.

DIRECTIONS From Exit 45 on I-81 near Marion, head south on VA 16 for 6.0 miles to the Jennings Visitor Center. From the Jennings Visitor Center, continue south on VA 16 for 9.4 miles to VA 741/Homestead Road, just beyond the Smyth–Grayson county line. Turn right on Homestead Road and follow it 0.4 mile to the Comers Creek Falls Trailhead, which will be on your right just past the bridge over Comers Creek.

GPS TRAILHEAD COORDINATES 36.711394, -81.474740

36 CHESTNUT CREEK FALLS
[2.0-mile out-and-back, easy]

The New River Trail, a railroad grade turned trail, leads you to this wide cascade. New River Trail State Park is Virginia's longest park, extending more than 57 miles along a former railbed. The rail-trail is the primary attraction, as it courses along a cinder bed and over trestles that span Chestnut Creek and the New River. Bicyclers are the primary users, though equestrians and hikers travel portions of the path. The trail demonstrates how, in our modern era, we can preserve scenic natural areas in the midst of human habitation.

The pretty trail follows the old railroad bed of the Norfolk and Western Railroad, beginning in the town of Galax. (It is an easy 11-mile out-and-back bike ride to Chestnut Creek Falls from the Galax trailhead.) The trail follows intimate Chestnut Creek, passing amid attractive woodlands, pasturelands, and a few houses. It eventually enters the wider New River Valley and stays there to its end. Occasional rapids and riverside bluffs satiate the visual palate.

For this hike, pick up the New River Trail at Chestnut Yard. Head south up the valley of Chestnut Creek. Woods envelop the trail, and elevation change is minimal. Bridge a few feeder creeks, coming to a trestle and Chestnut Creek Falls at 1.0 mile. The wide, 8-foot-high falls drop over a rock base at a bend in the creek. A ledge rises on the far side, fashioning an alluring pool. A little covered picnic shelter stands nearby.

CHESTNUT CREEK FALLS

The creek's namesake, the American chestnut, was once the dominant giant of the Southern Appalachians. This tree formerly ranged from Maine to Mississippi, and in southwest Virginia it grew to massive proportions. Its fruit was very important; chestnut acorns were a staple for everything from bears to birds. (Of course, humans eat them, too, as evidenced by the opening lyric to "The Christmas Song.")

DIRECTIONS From Exit 14 on I-77 at Hillsboro, take US 58 west 3.3 miles to turn right onto VA 620/Coulson Church Road. Drive 2.6 miles to turn left onto VA 707/Mount Zion Road. Follow Mount Zion Road 3.8 miles, then turn right on VA 635. Drive 1.6 miles, and finally turn left on VA 607/Iron Ridge Road. Follow it 1.5 miles to the Chestnut Yard access for New River Trail State Park.

GPS TRAILHEAD COORDINATES 36.723055, -80.916674

37 FALLS OF WILSON CREEK
[2.4-mile round-trip, moderate]

This raucous creek flows off Virginia's loftiest peaks at Mount Rogers National Recreation Area, displaying numerous cascades, including a pair of noteworthy cataracts that, although dissimilar, both have alluring plunge pools for swimmers on a hot summer day.

Leave near the state park campground gate on the Wilson Trail. You are starting at over 4,000 feet among red spruce and northern hardwoods on a steep descent. After a quarter mile, cross the roadlike Upchurch Road Trail. Begin curving upstream toward Wilson Creek, and reach the stream at 0.6 mile, near a storm shelter. Just below here, come to an old road and flat, a former bridge site crossing Wilson Creek. Find your first waterfall just below the old bridge crossing. This angled cascade tumbles about 12 feet into a huge, dusky plunge pool. Enjoy looks above and below of this spiller before returning to the singletrack Wilson Trail. Begin ascending along the streamside, where the path courses through rhododendron and around rock outcrops, with short side paths extending to lesser cataracts that will attract you too. The rocky trail continues to reach the top of a narrow, chutelike, 25-foot cascade at 1.1 miles, first making a wider sheet descent before narrowing into a long narrow crevice. Enjoy the top-down view from naked rock, then backtrack to the trail leading

Falls of Wilson Creek

to the base of the plunge pool, where you can savor a face-on view of this rugged spiller and perhaps swim above 4,000 feet in altitude.

DIRECTIONS From Exit 35 (Chilhowie) on I-81, take VA 107 for 11.4 miles to turn left onto VA 600. Stay on VA 600 for 8.1 miles to turn left on US 58. Follow US 58 east for 7.5 miles to turn left into Grayson Highlands State Park. Follow the main park road 3.3 miles, then turn right toward the park campground and Country Store. Follow this road 1.2 miles and park near the Country Store. The Wilson Creek Trail starts a few feet from the park campground entrance gate.

GPS TRAILHEAD COORDINATES 36.640090, -81.486725

38 FALLS OF CABIN CREEK
[1.9-mile loop, moderate]

This waterfall hike starts atop the heights of Grayson Highlands State Park, near heralded Massie Gap, where visitors seek to view the wild ponies of the Mount Rogers high country. After bagging these waterfalls on Cabin Creek, you might want to video a pony or two as well. The waterfalls on Cabin Creek are among the highest-elevation waterfalls in Virginia. From the parking lot at Massie Gap, join the signed singletrack Cabin Creek Trail as it enters thick woods and then crosses the state park's Horse Trail. The Cabin Creek Trail enters a hodgepodge of brush, grasses, and trees. Soon, traverse a dark rhododendron tunnel and cross a feeder stream of Cabin Creek, then reach the loop portion of the hike at 0.3 mile. Stay left and step over the feeder stream twice more in succession while dropping steeply amid red spruce and northern hardwoods.

The trail reaches Cabin Creek at 0.5 mile and then turns up this cool, clear highland waterway, passing a storm shelter. Come to the lower falls of Cabin Creek at 0.6 mile. First, you will encounter a 20-foot double-chute cascade with its streams coming together at the base. Another waterfall stands above this

FALLS OF CABIN CREEK

cataract, a narrow chute perhaps 18 feet high. These two cataracts are so close as to be a single spiller. You are already above 4,000 feet elevation and climbing. At 1.1 miles, keeps straight as the main trail splits right. Follow the zigzagging side trail a short piece along Cabin Creek to view a stairstep cascade, with a lowermost curtain drop of 10 feet. The entire pour-over is long, but because it consists of a succession of stairstep cascades, it's difficult to quantify its entire length.

To finish the loop, return to the main trail and pick up a nearly level railroad grade going left toward Massie Gap, coming alongside a fenceline. The railroad grade splits; stay with the lower grade and come to the beginning of the loop. Backtrack 0.3 mile to Massie Gap, returning to the trailhead at 1.9 mile.

DIRECTIONS From Exit 35 (Chilhowie) on I-81, take VA 107 for 11.4 miles to turn left onto VA 600. Drive 8.1 miles to turn left (east) on US 58. Follow US 58 east 7.5 miles to turn left into Grayson Highlands State Park. Follow the main park road 3.4 miles and you'll begin seeing parking for Massie Gap. Continue 0.1 mile then turn right on a paved park road. Turn right again into the original Massie Gap parking area. The Cabin Creek Trail starts in this smallish parking lot.

GPS TRAILHEAD COORDINATES 36.633868, -81.509865

39 ROWLAND CREEK FALLS
[3.4-mile round-trip, moderate]

This pretty waterfall hike starts in the wide lower valley of Rowland Creek, which becomes pinched in by rocky Chestnut Ridge. The hike then steepens and comes to Rowland Creek Falls, a 50-foot stairstep cascade.

Start the waterfall hike by following the orange-blazed Rowland Creek Trail away from Forest Road 643. Walk just a few feet before veering left onto an old woods road, upstream. Rowland Creek is off to the right. Continue heading up the wide flat to cross Rowland Creek at 0.3 mile. By 0.7 mile the hollow has narrowed. The large, mossy outcrops of Chestnut Ridge add a scenic touch to the valley. Pass a few warm-up cascades. At 1.2 miles, cross Rowland Creek again, then make two sharp switchbacks, again heading upstream, now on singletrack trail. Swing around a side hollow and return to the Rowland Creek valley, now on a precipitous ledge. Look for a side trail leading right, down to Rowland Creek

Falls at 1.7 miles. Numerous rock ledges lend a cascading effect to the falls. Use care when accessing the base of this long, tall cataract.

DIRECTIONS From Exit 44 on I-81 just south of Marion, take US 11 south for 2.2 miles. Just after cutting back under I-81, stay straight and join Adwolfe Road/VA 660. Follow Adwolfe Road 1.7 miles, then turn left onto Thomas Bridge Road. Follow it 1.7 miles and turn right onto South Fork Road. Follow South Fork Road 0.4 mile, then turn left onto Stoney Battery Road. Follow Stoney Battery Road 1.9 miles, then turn right onto Rowland Creek Lane. Follow Rowland Creek Lane 0.4 mile to enter Jefferson National Forest. Continue 0.1 mile to bridge Rowland Creek. Park on the left just after the road bridge crossing.

GPS TRAILHEAD COORDINATES 36.736028, -81.563250

ROWLAND CREEK FALLS

section three

North Carolina Waterfalls

CEDAR ROCK CREEK FALLS *(see Trip 74, page 159)*

Hanging Rock State Park

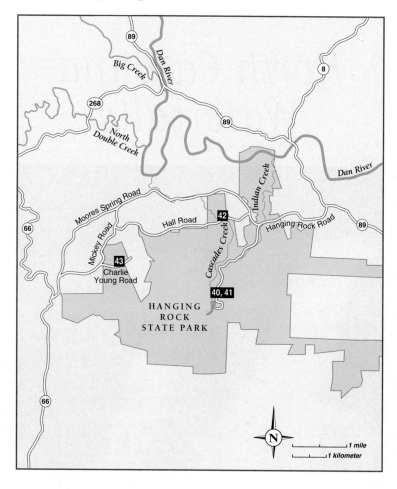

40 UPPER CASCADES
[0.4-mile out-and-back, easy]

Upper Cascades is the most easily reached waterfall in Hanging Rock State Park, via a wide all-access path from the visitor center. The path starts out paved but becomes gravel after passing the intersection with Rock Garden Trail. The trail to Upper Cascades is often used by rangers for summer interpretive programs.

On the way to the falls, a superb mountain view opens from an outcrop of rock overlooking Cascades Creek. The trail continues down to an elaborate wooden deck with three levels. Steps lead down from the platform to the edge of the creek. This gorge, like many steep ravines, escaped much of the logging in the 1930s. Some of the oldest trees in the park, including preserved giant hemlocks, can be seen below Upper Cascades.

UPPER CASCADES

The near-vertical Upper Cascades flows over a rocky drop that is 10 feet wide and 35 feet high. After sliding into a small pool below the falls, the stream squeezes through a gap between boulders and disappears. Downstream from the falls, after a series of short drops, Cascades Creek heads for Lower Cascades, which must be accessed separately, and eventually flows into the Dan River. Upstream from Upper Cascades, a dam built in 1938 impounds Cascade Creek as the park's 12-acre recreational lake.

DIRECTIONS From the junction of US 52 and US 421 in Winston-Salem, take US 52 north 0.75 mile to Exit 110B (US 311). Follow US 311 north 17 miles to NC 89. Keep straight on NC 89 west 9 miles to Hanging Rock Road. Turn left on Hanging Rock Road and follow it 1 mile to enter Hanging Rock State Park. Follow the road uphill to reach an intersection, and make a left turn toward the visitor center. The Upper Cascades Trail starts on the southwest side of the large visitor center parking area.

GPS TRAILHEAD COORDINATES 36.394050, -80.266925

41 HIDDEN FALLS AND WINDOW FALLS
[1.2-mile out-and-back, moderate]

Hidden Falls and Window Falls are on Indian Creek Trail, part of the state's longest path—the Mountains-to-Sea Trail. You can continue past the waterfalls, following the white blazes, for 3 miles along and across Indian Creek to the Dan River and beyond.

Leave the trailhead on a wide path, winding downhill in oak-dominated woods amid scads of mountain laurel, passing through a picnic area. After a few minutes of ridge walking, you begin to question whether this trail leads to a waterfall, as there is no water nearby. Then the path dips into the Indian Creek Gorge. The intonations of cascading water provide reassurance. It is your first destination—Hidden Falls. A spur trail leads right to this pour-over, which spills 16 feet over a dark rock face framed in greenery.

The path becomes more primitive beyond Hidden Falls and rolls over a stone slab before reaching a massive rock protrusion. Here, the main trail leaves left downhill to a geological feature where an eroded window-size hole opens astride Window Falls. The path then continues down more steps to the base of

WINDOW FALLS

Window Falls. Here, you can view the 24-foot, two-tiered cascade as well as the rock house below the falls and the stone promontory extending above the cataracts. Additionally, a narrow sliding cascade tumbles for 30 or 40 feet down a chute below the base of Window Falls.

> **DIRECTIONS** The Indian Creek Trail starts at the far end of the visitor center parking area. See Upper Cascades (page 99) for directions to the visitor center.
>
> **GPS TRAILHEAD COORDINATES** 36.395517, -80.265000

42 LOWER CASCADES
[0.8-mile out-and-back, easy]

Lower Cascades is the tallest and most spectacular waterfall in Hanging Rock State Park. It is on Cascades Creek, roughly 2 miles downstream from Upper Cascades. A series of 30-foot drops combine for a total drop of 120 feet.

The waterfall is at the northern boundary of the park in a 91-acre section between Hall Road and Moores Spring Road. This land became part of Hanging Rock in 1974 when it was bought from a local doctor, Spotswood Taylor, who owned several pieces of property adjacent to the park. Purportedly, Moravian botanist Lewis David von Schweinitz discovered the falls. Known as the father of American mycology, von Schweinitz also discovered approximately 1,500 species of plants near Hanging Rock and in the surrounding area.

The trail to Lower Cascades is a wide, easy track leading to the edge of a huge cliff, where you stand 100 feet above the gorge. The waterfall is almost directly beneath you. Please use caution in this area and do not venture too

LOWER CASCADES   *photo: Nicole Blouin*

close to the rocky edge. Fortunately, wooden steps and stone stairs lead to a view of the pour-over from its base.

At the turn of the 20th century, resorts developed north of the falls, on Moores Spring Road, to take advantage of two mineral springs. Until the late 1920s, Piedmont Springs and Moores Spring were popular destinations for those seeking the natural spring water.

DIRECTIONS From the junction of US 52 and US 421 in Winston-Salem, take US 52 north 0.75 mile to Exit 110B (US 311). Follow US 311 north 17 miles to NC 89. Keep straight on NC 89 west 9 miles to Hanging Rock Road. Turn left on Hanging Rock Road and continue 1.5 miles to turn right on Moores Spring Road. After 0.3 mile take a left onto Hall Road. Go 0.4 mile to the parking area for Lower Cascades, on the right (2143 Hall Road). The trailhead is at the upper end of the parking area.

GPS TRAILHEAD COORDINATES 36.414656, -80.264869

43 TORY'S DEN FALLS
[0.6-mile out-and-back, moderate]

Tory's Den Falls gets its name from a Revolutionary War legend about the 20-foot-deep cave near the waterfall. As with many legends, the story changes with the storyteller, but all the old tales involving Tory's Den describe the cave as a refuge for those loyal to England during the Revolutionary War, known as Tories.

We like to share the story about C. Jack Martin's daughter. Martin wanted to break free from English rule, and he lived about 15 miles from the cave during the Revolutionary era. His daughter was captured by the Tories, held for ransom, and hidden in the cave. Whether she was rescued because smoke was seen coming from the cave or because a piece of material from her torn petticoat was found, the story has a happy ending.

From Tory's Den Trail, you can visit the cave and the waterfall. Leave the large trailhead on a narrow path. The path crosses a creek and then takes wood-and-earth steps. You will come to a sign indicating that Tory's Den is to the right (descend 100 yards to the cave, which is about 20 by 10 feet with a sloping roof) and that Tory's Den Falls is to the left—about 25 yards. The trail leads down steps to the rim of the gorge.

TORY'S DEN FALLS

Tory's Den Falls is a delicate waterfall; a tiny creek spills over a series of rock terraces. The current is only 5 feet wide at the precipice, but then it divides and falls, and divides and falls again, getting wider with each drop. From where you stand, on the edge of a cliff opposite the main portion of the waterfall, you can see about 30 feet of Tory's Den Falls. Small trees and holly bushes push up between rocks around the falls. The creek continues to drop on its way down the valley to the Dan River. A good view of the surrounding hills can be gained near the top of the falls.

DIRECTIONS From the junction of US 52 and US 421 in Winston-Salem, take US 52 north 0.75 mile to Exit 110B (US 311). Follow US 311 north 17 miles to NC 89. Keep straight on NC 89 west 9 miles to Hanging Rock Road. Turn left on Hanging Rock Road and continue 1.5 miles to turn right on Moores Spring Road. After 0.3 mile take a left onto Hall Road. Travel 2.4 miles to Mickey Road and turn left. After 0.4 mile turn left onto Charlie Young Road and drive 0.5 mile to a parking lot. The trailhead is marked with a wooden sign.

GPS TRAILHEAD COORDINATES 36.401801, -80.299581

Stone Mountain State Park and Doughton Park

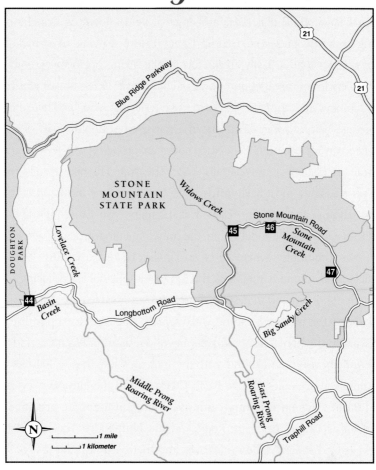

44 BASIN CREEK FALLS
[8.4-mile round-trip, difficult]

Basin Creek flows off the Blue Ridge at a tract of land known as Doughton Park, coursing near the preserved Caudill Cabin before flowing over rock in the 20-foot cataract that is Basin Creek Falls. While hiking up to this scenic spiller, you will view lesser cascades and pools of chilly Basin Creek, above which stand many chimneys and homesites of Basin Cove residents, who lived here a century or more ago before being wiped out in a massive flood. Now part of the Blue Ridge Parkway's Doughton Park, the mountain property is a jewel harboring both human history and waterfalls. *Note:* The waterfall hike entails multiple bridgeless crossings, most likely fords; thus, it is best done from spring through autumn. Though the falls are reached at 4.2 miles, you can continue 0.7 mile farther to see the intact Caudill Cabin, the only remaining structure of the former Basin Cove community, where 20 or so families resided until July 1916, when torrential and continuous rains raised Basin Creek to lethal levels, killing most of its residents. Shocked and in despair, those who survived left the valley for good.

Leaving the trailhead, ascend gated Grassy Gap Fire Road past the Cedar Ridge Trail on the right. Soon you walk beyond a dam on Basin Creek. Though the mountains rise high around you, the trek rises less than 1,000 feet in the first 4 miles. At 1.7 miles, bridge Basin Creek to find the attractive, evergreen-shaded Basin Cove backcountry campsite. Soon join the more primitive Basin Creek Trail as Grassy Gap Fire Road and the Bluff Ridge Trail split left. The richly vegetated stream hollow narrows, and then you find the first of several homesite chimneys at 2.4 miles. Other homesite evidence includes rock piles and walls, level spots, and perennial flower plantings such as jonquils. Begin crossing Basin Creek. At 3.2 miles, look right (you are on the left-hand bank heading upstream) for a 20-foot slide waterfall below. Accessing this cataract is very difficult and is best done by coming up the creek from downstream.

At 4.2 miles, now on the right-hand bank heading upstream, come to 20-foot Basin Creek Falls. Here, the stream pours over gray stone, slows, and makes a second, lesser drop before slowing in a crystalline pool framed in rhododendron. Its base is an easy scramble. If you want to see the Caudill Cabin, continue 0.7 mile to a clearing where the rustic log structure stands.

BASIN CREEK FALLS

Families lived there just short of 30 years before abandoning the home two years after the devastating 1916 flood.

> **DIRECTIONS** From mile 242 on the Blue Ridge Parkway near Laurel Springs, take NC 18 south 6.2 miles to turn left on Longbottom Road. Follow it 6.4 miles to cross a bridge over Basin Creek. The parking area is on the right side of Longbottom Road, while the trail is on the left.
>
> **GPS TRAILHEAD COORDINATES** 36.375250, -81.144778

45 WIDOW'S CREEK FALLS
[0.2-mile out-and-back, easy]

You'll be pleased to discover the walk to 30-foot Widow's Creek Falls is a short distance on a relatively flat trail.

Widow's Creek Trail, which heads out from the backcountry parking lot past the bridge, leads to six backpacker sites. These sites along Widow's Creek

WIDOW'S CREEK FALLS *photo: Nicole Blouin*

require a 1.5- to 3-mile hike. Each primitive campsite accommodates four people and requires a permit and a small fee.

Stone Mountain State Park owns the entire watershed of Widow's Creek. The headwaters for the creek are just south of the Blue Ridge Parkway. The creek is one of several in the park that comprise 17 miles of designated trout waters. Widow's Creek flows into the regularly stocked East Prong of Roaring River. The water drops about 25 feet over a rock slab into a greenish-blue pool and then pushes on over smaller shoals.

DIRECTIONS From the Blue Ridge Parkway, exit at milepost 229.7 to head east on US 21 toward Elkin. Travel 3 miles to Roaring Gap and turn right on Oklahoma Road. It is then 3 miles to the park. From the visitor center, follow the main road 3.5 miles. Pull over in the backcountry parking lot past the bridge.

GPS TRAILHEAD COORDINATES 36.398077, -81.051126

46 STONE MOUNTAIN FALLS

[4.5-mile loop, strenuous]

In the 1960s, R. Philip Hanes Jr. (former CEO of the Hanes clothing company) saw a lot of trash go over the waterfalls here while he was on a picnic. To protect the falls, he decided to purchase them. The tract was the first piece of land that Hanes bought in the area. He eventually donated more than 1,000 acres to Stone Mountain State Park, and this area was the last portion he contributed. Stone Mountain Falls became part of the park in 1986.

This cataract was not always called Stone Mountain Falls. Old maps reveal other names, including Beauty Falls and Deer Falls. Here is a strange story about

STONE MOUNTAIN FALLS

the latter: Sometimes deer that try to drink from Big Sandy Creek slip and tumble over the falls to their death. Early residents saw opportunity in this misfortune. Families were assigned different mornings to claim any deer at the base of the falls. Although a ranger assured us that the park does not lose too many deer in this manner, one lay at the edge of the pool on one of our visits.

The Stone Mountain Loop Trail is your ticket to Stone Mountain View, Stone Mountain Falls, the preserved Hutchinson Homestead, and the summit of Stone Mountain. Pick up the loop at the park's Lower Trailhead. The circuit takes you through an open meadow and past the south face of the mountain. After entering the woods, you will hike a ridge to the falls. The last part of the trail takes you across the dome and down the other side to the parking area.

Stone Mountain View, within the first 0.5 mile of the hike, is a grassy meadow at the base of the south face, and is also home to the Hutchinson Homestead. A plaque describes the dome as a registered natural landmark. Spread a blanket or relax on the bench. Watch the climbers struggle up routes with names such as Sufficiently Breathless and No Alternative, near where feral goats used to effortlessly traverse the exposed sloping rock.

At Stone Mountain Falls, you can observe a 200-foot sheet of falling water as it slides down a near-vertical broad granite slab. The falls are on Big Sandy Creek, which actually drops a total of 500 feet. Be sure to walk out to the pool at the base before starting the hike up the side of the waterfall.

About 300 steps make up the elaborate staircase adjacent to the falls. This man-made segment of trail ascends the east shoulder of Stone Mountain, along-side the falls and all the way to the top. Decades back, before the trail was improved, hikers went from tree to tree, climbing eroded switchbacks.

After visiting Stone Mountain Falls, pass the spur trail to the Upper Trail-head. (Many hikers will be taking a shorter out-and-back route to the falls that starts from the Upper Trailhead, located at the park visitor center.) You reach the summit of Stone Mountain (2,305´) about 2 miles into the hike, after the 0.5-mile, steep incline. On top, there are sections of bare rock, lined on the edges with pine and cedar and sparsely covered with moss and lichen. These naked rock faces offer first-rate panoramas. Look north to view the Blue Ridge and southwest to view Cedar Rock. Views like this are what make the Stone Mountain Loop the better hiking choice than the direct route to the falls from the Upper Trailhead.

DIRECTIONS To reach Stone Mountain State Park from the Blue Ridge Parkway, exit at milepost 229.7 to head east on US 21 toward Elkin. Travel 3 miles to Roaring Gap and turn right on Oklahoma Road. It is then 3 miles to the park. From the visitor center, follow the main road 2.5 miles to the large, paved parking area on the left, where you will find the trailhead and restrooms.

GPS TRAILHEAD COORDINATES 36.398077, -81.051126

47 MIDDLE FALLS AND LOWER FALLS
[3.4-mile out-and-back, moderate]

When we headed off to visit Middle Falls and Lower Falls, our first question was, "Where is Upper Falls?" The answer: Upper Falls is another name for Stone Mountain Falls. All three waterfalls are on Big Sandy Creek. Middle Falls is about 0.5 mile downstream from Stone Mountain Falls, and Lower Falls is about 0.5 mile downstream from Middle Falls.

Middle and Lower Falls are accessed from the Stone Mountain Loop Trail on a side trail—an old roadbed that crosses Big Sandy Creek several times. (You

LOWER FALLS

may have to wade if the water is high.) To reach the trailhead, follow the Stone Mountain Loop Trail from the Lower Trailhead about 1.3 miles to a sign indicating the side trail to Middle and Lower Falls, not surprisingly named the Middle Falls/Lower Falls Trail. Take it 0.2 mile to a 0.1-mile spur leading to Middle Falls, a slide cascade difficult to view face-on without getting your feet wet. Then return to the trail junction and continue 0.5 mile downstream to Lower Falls, near the southern boundary of the park. If you want to combine a hike to Middle and Lower Falls with the loop to Stone Mountain Falls, count on a total of 5.4 miles. You can also come to the falls from the east side of the Stone Mountain Loop, beginning at the Upper Trailhead, accessed via a connector from the park visitor center. If you go to Middle and Lower Falls, it is about 3 miles out-and-back from the Upper Trailhead, and you can see Stone Mountains Falls along the way.

Middle Falls is a series of small cascades, with one section that slides about 30 feet at a 30-degree angle into a large swimming hole. Lower Falls is similar but somewhat steeper, sliding 25 feet over a smooth dome. Big Sandy Creek narrows beyond the shallow pool; you can jump across the creek to a rock beach covered with colorful, palm-size stones.

Many youth programs bring kids to Stone Mountain State Park and bypass the recognized highlights: Stone Mountain Falls and the summit of Stone Mountain. Instead, they head for Lower Falls wearing old bathing suits or cutoffs. Sailing down the sliding falls is part of their organized activity. We're surprised Lower Falls doesn't have a more suitable name as do other natural waterslides in the Blue Ridge—say, Sliding Rock Falls or Bust-Yer-Butt Falls.

DIRECTIONS To reach Stone Mountain State Park from the Blue Ridge Parkway, exit at milepost 229.7 to head east on US 21 toward Elkin. Travel 3 miles to Roaring Gap and turn right on Oklahoma Road. It is then 3 miles to the park. From the visitor center, travel the main road 2.5 miles to the parking area for Stone Mountain Loop Trail. The Middle Falls/Lower Falls Trail is 1.3 miles into the Stone Mountain Loop Trail on the right, where a wooden sign indicates Middle and Lower Falls.

GPS TRAILHEAD COORDINATES 36.398077, -81.051126

Blowing Rock

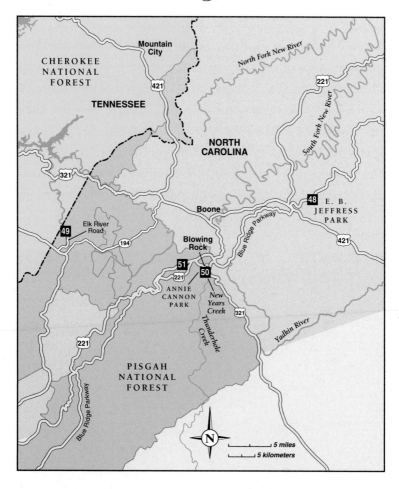

48 CASCADES

[0.8-mile loop, easy]

"Water . . . like liquid lace from overhead . . . dashes past to swirl and slide downward in an abandon of spray and foam ripples." The quote is from a plaque near the top of the Cascades, and the description is accurate because the narrow, 240-foot waterfall rolls and rushes past you, rather than falling at your feet. The waters from Falls Creek are bound for the ocean at Winyah Bay, South Carolina, after flowing into the Yadkin River, which in turn flows into the Pee Dee River.

The Cascades is at E. B. Jeffress Park, 600 mountainous acres honoring a man who loved this land. Jeffress was chairman of the North Carolina highway

CASCADES

CASCADES

department in the early 1930s. He fought hard in favor of building the proposed Blue Ridge Parkway through North Carolina. The waterfall is just one piece of a natural scenic mosaic. Enjoy a pleasant walk on the self-guided Cascades Nature Trail. Informative displays along the way provide information about the flora. Learn when flowers bloom, where certain plants live, and which trees the mountaineers used for what—knowledge you can carry with you on any waterfall hike in the Blue Ridge.

To follow the loop counterclockwise, bear right at each of the forks. The trail follows Falls Creek through a dense hardwood forest, crosses the creek on a wooden bridge near the top of the Cascades, and then heads down a well-built walkway that hugs the side of the waterfall. The upper platform is at the brink, and the lower platform is partway down. Retrace your steps up the stairs and look for the RETURN TRAIL sign.

DIRECTIONS From downtown Blowing Rock, head north on the Blue Ridge Parkway to E. B. Jeffress Park, located at milepost 271.9. The trailhead is just beyond the restrooms.

GPS TRAILHEAD COORDINATES 36.249983, -81.456850

49 ELK FALLS
[0.5-mile out-and-back, easy]

No one knows how deep the pool is at the bottom of this waterfall. The Elk River drops 50 feet over a wide, even ledge to form Elk River Falls and then crashes into a huge rock bowl that looks like an amphitheater. Divers going down with weights have not been able to fight the force pushing upward. There are several stories of bags of silver being dropped into the pool during the Civil War.

Like many place-names in the mountains, the river and falls honor the Eastern elk, a great animal that inhabited the area when wildlands stretched across the Southern Appalachians. A relic of the most recent ice age, the elk was the largest member of the deer family (weighing 500–1,000 pounds) and was often confused with the moose. Elk, called *wapiti* by the American Indians, were last seen in the Blue Ridge in the early 1800s. They have since been successfully reintroduced to the Southern Appalachians in the Cataloochee area of the Smokies, as well as the northern Cumberland Plateau of East Tennessee and Kentucky.

There is a story about a woman who lived on the Elk River about 9 miles from the falls but thought she was in Kentucky. It was 1825 when Delilah Baird of Valle Crucis eloped with Johnny Holtzclaw, who was supposed to take her to his property in Kentucky. Three years passed, and one day when Delilah was out gathering ginseng, she found some of her father's cattle and discovered that she was only 8 miles from home. Delilah reunited with her family but then returned to her "Kentucky" home.

ELK FALLS   *photo: Kevin Adams*

Elk Falls is located in the Elk Falls Recreation Area of Pisgah National Forest, and the area is a wonderful place to spend a day. You can swim or fish, and tables along the river above the falls offer great picnic spots.

Note: The falls can get very crowded during summer weekends. Also, this is when you will see people jumping off the falls—a classic Southern Appalachian "Hey, y'all, watch this!" moment. People are injured here regularly, and local paramedics can drive to the falls blindfolded. Avoid swimming below the falls when the water is running high, as the currents are incredibly strong. However, the beauty of the natural setting cannot be denied, as the cataract descends 50 feet over a granite ledge. Large rock slabs provide repose points below the falls.

DIRECTIONS From the intersection of US 19E and NC 194 west of Blowing Rock, take US 19E west into Elk Park. About 0.2 mile north of town, turn right at the sign for Elk Falls. After 0.3 mile, turn left onto Elk River Road and follow it 3.5 miles to Elk Falls parking.

GPS TRAILHEAD COORDINATES 36.197350, -81.970123

50 WATERFALLS ON THE GLEN BURNEY TRAIL

🌢 **Cascades** [1.4-mile out-and-back, easy–moderate]
🌢 **Glen Burney Falls** [2.2-mile out-and-back, moderate]
🌢 **Glen Mary Falls** [2.6-mile out-and-back, moderate]

When you look for waterfalls, the setting is rarely downtown. Well, Glen Burney Trail is just off Main Street in Blowing Rock. From the trailhead in town, at a city park, you can hike to three falls on New Years Creek. Annie Cannon Park includes a walking trail around Mayview Lake, as well as playground equipment, all just across the street from the Glen Burney Trail parking area.

The town owned a half acre, and the Cannon family contributed $100,000 to develop the land into a park. Annie Ludlow Cannon, wife of J. W. Cannon of Cannon Textile Industry, taught Sunday school for years and did extensive social work, helping start the Community Club and supporting the Grandfather Home for Children. She was a true friend to the town of Blowing Rock.

Another notable friend of Blowing Rock was Emily Pruden, a schoolteacher who donated the land around the waterfalls to be preserved as part of the park. Circa 1900, she started the Skyland Academy, a boarding school for underprivileged children. A marker at the south end of town commemorates her benevolence.

GLEN MARY FALLS

CASCADES

The Glen Burney Trail is not new. Old-timers say it has been around as long as they can remember—more than a century. After passing the sewage pump station, the trail descends into the Glen Burney Gorge. Find some ruins from the early 1920s of a nonmechanical, gravity-flow wastewater plant that served the Mayview Manor Hotel, which was torn down in 1978. For its time, the plant was extremely sensitive to the environment.

After a half mile, a wooden bridge spans New Years Creek. You are now descending along the left bank of the creek. At 0.7 mile, reach the Cascades, a 30-foot cataract bounding over rocks and chutes. Continue down along New Years Creek, avoiding closed accesses. After passing a top-down, partly obscured view of Glen Burney Falls at 1.1 miles, a side path takes you to the bottom of the falls, where you can gain a face-on look at this 50-foot-tall and -wide stony slide that becomes sheer at the drop's end. The trail descends farther, moderated by switchbacks, to find the last and largest waterfall, Glen Mary Falls, at 1.3 miles. You'll pass by the upper part of the falls first, where a

GLEN BURNEY FALLS

rocky outcrop affords a nice view before making the base of the long, tiered falls. Rest up for the 600-foot climb back out.

> **DIRECTIONS** In downtown Blowing Rock, turn west off Main Street onto Laurel Lane. At the four-way stop (Wallingford Street), continue straight. Just before the bridge, turn left into Annie Cannon Park. The trailhead is just beyond the information board.

> **GPS TRAILHEAD COORDINATES** 36.132710, -81.680514

51 BOONE FORK FALLS
[5.4-mile loop, strenuous]

The falls along this stream astride the Blue Ridge Parkway are scenic in and of themselves. They are enhanced by the celebrated Boone name and a forest that was cut by one famous person and bought by another, all along a loop hike that is one of the best along the entire Blue Ridge Parkway.

BOONE FORK FALLS

The falls are on Boone Fork, named after Daniel Boone's nephew, Jesse. Ol' Jesse had a cabin and a small farm near the creek in the early 1800s. The huge tract of virgin chestnut, poplar, and hemlock was timbered in the early 1900s by William S. Whiting, a great lumber baron. Julian Price, founder of Jefferson Standard Life (now merged with Lincoln Financial), one of the nation's major insurance companies, purchased the land in the late 1930s to use as a retreat for his employees. Price was killed in an automobile crash, and the land was donated to the National

Park Service. Boone Fork was dammed to form Price Lake, a memorial to a man who deeply loved these parts.

Julian Price Park, one of the most popular recreation areas on the Parkway, was dedicated in 1960. It consists of 4,200 acres of mountain land, ranging in elevation from 3,400 to 4,000 feet. In addition to hiking, you can enjoy the campground, a picnic area, and a lake.

The hiking on this loop can be slow on the rocky path along lower Boone Fork, where you will find unusually christened Hebron Colony Falls (named for the colony of large rocks in Boone Fork). However, the second part of the circuit—up Bee Tree Creek—is more foot-friendly. After bridging Boone Fork at the picnic area, head right, downstream along Boone Fork as it meanders through field and woods, passing the lower picnic area. At 0.6 mile, bridge a side stream of Boone Fork. At 1.2 miles, the Mountains-to-Sea Trail leaves right across a bridge, then you reach small falls, beaches, and pools popular with visitors. At 1.7 miles, take the spur right to Hebron Colony Falls, where you find a colossal colony of boulders through which Boone Fork works its way in seemingly every conceivable form of cataract and pool. There is no single fall but rather an aggregation of cascades you can visit by boulder-hopping through the colony.

Back on the Boone Fork Trail, you'll enter rocky terrain, even using a ladder to continue at one point. At 2.1 miles, reach a pair of drops and pools sometimes known as Boone Fork Falls. Here the stream makes rocky drops over 40 feet in a thickly vegetated, cool canyon. At 2.6 miles, turn up Bee Tree Creek. Rock-hop it more than a dozen times before bisecting an open meadow and trekking through Price Park Campground to reach the trailhead.

DIRECTIONS From milepost 296.4 on the Blue Ridge Parkway, about 3.7 miles west of Blowing Rock, turn into the Julian Price Picnic Area, and park near the restrooms. Look for a sign just beyond the building, directing you across Boone Fork Creek to the trailhead at the information board and map.

GPS TRAILHEAD COORDINATES 36.139568, -81.727427

Linville

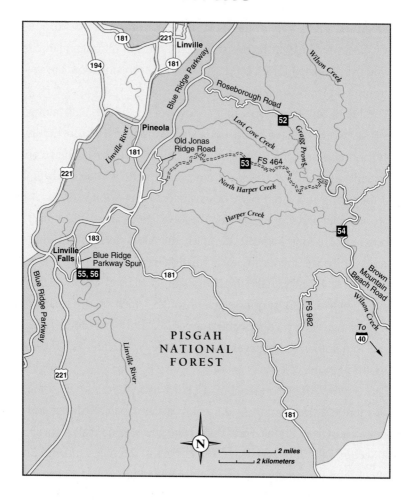

52 HUNT FISH FALLS AND FALLS OF GRAGG PRONG
[6.0-mile out-and-back, moderate]

This best-for-summer trek is about more than waterfalls; it's also about getting in the water. In addition to exciting cataracts, hikers here can enjoy superlative swimming holes. The Mountains-to-Sea Trail (MST) is your earthen conduit to explore this watery part of the Pisgah National Forest. First, you will trace Gragg Prong, with its waterfalls and slide cascades. Turn up Lost Cove Creek to find popular Hunt Fish Falls, a double drop with a tributary pour-over at the same point. A huge granite-lined swimming hole lies at the base of the falls and is often touted as the best swimming hole in the Carolina mountains. Besides swimming, wet-footed creek crossings provide another reason to go in summer.

This area was once proposed as the greater Lost Cove Wilderness. Despite no such designation, the area is de facto wildland. Take the MST as it crosses a crystalline tributary. The path descends the right bank of smallish Gragg Prong. Unpredictably big pools slow between rapids, and occasional little islands divide the stream as it pulses. Descend beneath evergreen arbors on the tight valley slope.

Rock-hop Gragg Prong three times before arriving at a gray granite slab and a set of cascades stairstepping into alternating pools at 1.2 miles. The stairstep cataract drops an aggregate 50 feet. Hikers leave the trail for open rock

HUNT FISH FALLS

slabs. At 1.4 miles, a spur leads right to another impressive five-tiered slide cascade dropping a good 40 feet. From the top of the falls, you can gaze down granite-walled Gragg Prong.

Cross Gragg Prong at 2.0 miles and reach Lost Cove Creek at 2.2 miles. Turn right with the MST. At 2.3 miles, the Timber Ridge Trail leaves right, but you split left with the MST, rock-hopping Lost Cove Creek at 2.4 miles. Bisect a wide, piney camping flat, and then ascend to the rock slab of Hunt Fish Falls at 3.0 miles. The cataract makes two quick drops followed by a slide, both modest in height. Hunt Fish Falls is more about the huge swimming pool. The still water, lined in rock, is deep, wide, and long. It is hard to believe that pools of this size are found in streams as small as Gragg Prong and Lost Cove Creek.

DIRECTIONS From milepost 308 on the Blue Ridge Parkway near Linville (16 miles southwest of Blowing Rock), take Roseboro Road 4.8 miles east to the bridge over Gragg Prong. The trail starts on the right bank as you face downstream.

GPS TRAILHEAD COORDINATES 36.031791, -81.803398

53 NORTH HARPER FALLS
[2.4-mile out-and-back, easy]

This is one of the most enthralling falls on the Blue Ridge, and you can soak in a little pioneer history at the hike's beginning. A drop of a little more than 200 feet makes this out-and-back hike easy; furthermore, the hike to the falls is dry, making it doable in any season, unlike other falls in the greater Harper Creek area that require wet fords. Initially, the trail to the falls traces an old forest road past a mountaineer homesite a short distance into the walk. Continuing down, you reach the imposing granite slope that is North Harper Falls, a wide-open, 200-foot stream spill that first cartwheels as a long slide, culminating in an archetypal drop and pool. Mountain vistas enhance the watery splendor. It takes a few minutes to absorb the entirety of this cataract.

The North Harper Falls Trail descends from Long Ridge and Forest Road 464. (The Little Lost Cliffs Trail leads right and uphill and offers stellar views of its own.) Follow the old forest road under oaks, maples, and pines, keeping an

North Harper Falls

eye peeled left for the standing chimney of an old homesite. Investigate the area for stone foundations, metal artifacts, and a spring. An easy downhill wanders in and out of shallow coves where tributaries dribble down hollows divided by drier ridges, ever deeper into the North Harper Creek valley.

At 1.0 mile, you will come to North Harper Creek Trail. Turn right here on a singletrack path, walking under mountain laurel well above North Harper Creek. Ahead, spur trails lead to lower North Harper Falls, but hold your horses and stay on the marked trail until 1.2 miles, where a well-used path leads left to topmost North Harper Falls. From this vantage, the falls seemingly curve into oblivion over steepening bedrock. This same treeless stone slab opens views of Simmons Ridge and mountains beyond. To see the rest of the falls, you must head downstream. Unless recent rains have made the stream high, you can simply walk the dry bedrock beside North Harper Creek. However, if the rock is wet or the water high, use spur trails to access the lower falls. The lower portion of North Harper Falls morphs to an almost sheer drop of 40 feet, slowing its 200-foot drop in a rhododendron-shrouded pool.

DIRECTIONS From milepost 311.3 on the Blue Ridge Parkway south of Linville (about 19 miles southwest of Blowing Rock), head south on Old

Jonas Ridge Road/NC 1518, and drive 1.7 miles to Long Ridge Baptist Church on the left. Turn left on gravel FR 464. After 3.1 miles, you will pass the first Little Lost Cliffs western trailhead. Continue 1.3 miles and reach the Little Lost Cliffs eastern trailhead and the North Harper Falls Trail on your right.

GPS TRAILHEAD COORDINATES 36.010267, -81.825583

54 FALLS OF HARPER CREEK

⬥ **Harper Creek Falls** [2.8-mile out-and-back, easy–moderate]
⬥ **South Harper Falls Loop** [9.4-mile loop, strenuous]

This hike has two distinct options. You can make an easy, dry-footed trek to Harper Creek Falls or tackle a challenging loop to a second waterfall—South Harper Falls—enjoyed from multiple vantage points, including a vista that takes in not only the cataract but also Grandfather Mountain and the crest of the Blue Ridge.

First, make a 1.4-mile well-trampled hike to double-decker, deep-pooled, granite-lined Harper Creek Falls. If you choose to go on, you'll leave the crowds behind, crisscrossing Harper Creek to meet South Harper Creek. More fords lead to South Harper Creek Falls, a 200-foot slide encircled by a stone amphitheater. Ascend past the falls to take in an all-encompassing view of this cataract from an outcrop, enhanced by the Blue Ridge skyline beyond. Your return trip descends Raider Camp Creek valley. Make no mistake: the route beyond Harper Creek Falls can be demanding, but the rewards exceed the challenges of the narrow trail and multiple fords. If the water is high, just visit Harper Creek Falls, as the ensuing fords may prove too much.

SOUTH HARPER FALLS

HARPER CREEK FALLS

From the trailhead, the slender Harper Creek Trail winds uphill in thick woods with nary a creek in sight. At 0.2 mile, top out in a gap. The Yellow Buck Mountain Trail leaves right, but you stay straight on the Harper Creek Trail, working downhill in evergreens. At 1.1 miles, come to the Raider Camp Trail, which runs in conjunction with the Mountains-to-Sea Trail (MST). Stay right, heading uphill with the Harper Creek Trail–MST. (If you make the entire falls loop, Raider Camp Trail will be the return route.) The Harper Creek Trail–MST splits at 1.3 miles. To reach Harper Creek Falls, stay left with the level logging grade. You will soon hear two-tiered Harper Creek Falls dropping 30 feet, then 15 feet, into respective granite bathtubs. It is a steep drop to the falls, but a thick rope tied to a tree allows hikers to reach them in midcataract. This is a popular swimming hole and your turnaround point for the easy hike.

To make the loop, backtrack, rejoining the Harper Creek Trail–MST, heading upstream on an exponentially less-used path. Rich woods tower overhead, and vegetation grows on anything not moving. Ford Harper Creek at 2.3, 2.5, and 2.8 miles, coming to an easy-to-miss intersection at 3.6 miles. Here, the orange-blazed Harper Creek Trail leaves left, fording Harper Creek, and the blue-blazed North Harper Creek Trail keeps straight along the river-bank. The MST, with its circular white dot, joins North Harper Creek Trail. Go left on the Harper Creek Trail, fording Harper Creek at a big pool where Harper Creek and North Harper Creek merge.

The next seven crossings of Harper Creek will be fun in summertime at normal flows, but the trail can be overgrown. Thus far, the hiking has been easy, with a mere 100-foot-per-mile gradient. That is about to change. At 4.9 miles, the gradients of the Harper Creek Trail and creek sharpen. Switchback uphill as the rock maw of Harper Creek opens. South Harper Creek Falls crashes through the trees. Spur paths leave left to view the cavernous pour-over along its 200-foot double drop.

Reach the top of the falls and open rock at 5.2 miles. Look back at the stone gorge below. It is hard to capture the entire falls unless you continue to the vantage point ahead. Pay close attention: the trail splits, but stay left, joining the Raider Camp Trail. Walk along Harper Creek, and then cross it left at a stream bend. Beyond the crossing, turn left, switchbacking uphill. At 5.5 miles, meet a roadbed and stay left, descending to an overlook of South Harper Creek Falls. This pine-rimmed rock outcrop reveals stellar vistas near and far. Below, South Harper Creek Falls spills into its granite funnel, which is longer than it looks from up close. Northward, the resplendent heights of Grandfather Mountain and the Blue Ridge form a wooded wall. This is a place to linger.

Rejoin the Raider Camp Trail, and again meet the MST. Head left on an easy, wide path. At 6.5 miles, the MST bisects a gap and descends to Raider Camp Creek. Continue a downward trek to reach Harper Creek. Make the last ford, entering a flat with campsites and user-created trails. Reach a trail junction and Harper Creek Trail at 8.3 miles, completing the circuit. From here, backtrack 1.1 miles to the trailhead.

DIRECTIONS From I-40, take Exit 103 for Morganton and turn onto US 64 East. Continue 0.7 mile, then turn left on US 64 Truck East, also signed as US 64 Bypass. Follow US 64 Truck East for 2.2 miles, then turn left on NC 181 North. Follow NC 181 North for 11.3 miles to Brown Mountain Beach Road. Turn right and drive 5.0 miles to turn left, staying with Brown Mountain Beach Road (the road going straight becomes Adako Road). Look for a national forest sign indicating Mortimer Campground at this intersection. Follow Brown Mountain Beach Road 7.1 more miles, and the parking area will be on your left.

GPS TRAILHEAD COORDINATES 35.977517, -81.766233

55 LINVILLE FALLS

- ◊ **Falls Trail** [1.6-mile out-and-back, easy]
- ◊ **Gorge Trail** [1.4-mile out-and-back, strenuous]
- ◊ **Plunge Basin Trail** [1.0-mile out-and-back, moderate]

Instead of several waterfalls on one trail, the Linville Falls area offers multiple trails to one waterfall, with a total of six viewpoints. Download a map at nps.gov /blri/planyourvisit/linville-falls-trails.htm, or take a picture of the trailhead map at the Linville Falls Visitor Center. Hosting thousands of visitors annually, Linville Falls is probably the most famous waterfall on the Blue Ridge Parkway and was designated a Natural Heritage Area in 1989.

Linville Falls is a double cascade with a vanishing act between the two falls. The upper falls are wide and gentle, pouring over several shelves for a total of 15 feet. Here, the river is lazy. Suddenly it disappears into a narrow channel. Out of sight, it dives 60 feet through a winding chamber before reappearing as the lower falls, a thunderous 45-foot drop and the largest-volume waterfall in the Blue Ridge. The force of this powerful river has shaped a large

LINVILLE FALLS

basin with towering cliffs. The river flows out of the pool, leaves the recreation area, and enters the Linville Gorge Wilderness.

The headwaters of the Linville River are on Grandfather Mountain, and the river flows to the Catawba Valley through one of the most rugged gorges in the country, Linville Gorge. The sheer rock walls of Linville Mountain (west) and Jonas Ridge (east) confine the water for 12 miles while it descends 2,000 feet. The difference in elevation between the rim and river is about 1,500 feet.

The Cherokee called the area Eeseeoh, which means "river of cliffs." Settlers called the river and the falls Linville to honor the explorer William Linville, who in 1766 was attacked and killed in the gorge by American Indians. In 1952 John D. Rockefeller donated the cascade tract to the National Park Service. The 440-acre area offers picnic sites, a small visitor center, and a campground. Rangers conduct interpretive programs, including campfire talks and guided nature walks. An information shelter provides a large map of the trail system directing you to the Falls, Gorge, and Plunge Basin Trails.

The Falls Trail is the most popular route to view the cataracts. Four overlooks along the rim of the gorge present a variety of perspectives: First Overlook (upper falls), Chimney View (the chimney-shaped rock for which the viewpoint was named and the first look at the lower falls), Gorge View (the river cutting through the mountains), and Erwins View (the spectacular gorge and a distant view of the falls).

The Gorge Trail is our favorite because it goes to the bottom, face-to-face with this magnificent waterfall. Only from the river's edge can one fully appreciate the grandeur of any gorge.

The Plunge Basin Trail, which descends about one-third of the way into the basin, is the shortest route to view the lower falls. This unusual overlook is a rocky platform jutting out from the hillside—like balcony seats at a great performance.

DIRECTIONS Leave Linville and head south on US 221 to Pineola. Take NC 181 heading south about 2 miles, and access the Blue Ridge Parkway on the left. Travel south to milepost 316.4, and turn left onto the 1.4-mile spur road that leads to Linville Falls. Signs lead the way to the falls.

GPS TRAILHEAD COORDINATES 35.953700, -81.926533

56 DUGGERS CREEK FALLS

[0.3-mile loop, easy]

Duggers Creek Falls is one of the smallest named falls in the Blue Ridge. The creek flows through a narrow chute as it enters the tiny canyon and spills over a 10-foot ledge. The surrounding rock walls are 15 feet apart at the bridge (and waterfall observation point) but only 3 feet apart at the falls. Duggers Creek flows down Jonas Ridge and into the Linville River.

The trail begins in a tunnel of rhododendrons that leads you over to Duggers Creek. Cross on the wooden bridge, climb two short sets of stone steps, and immediately descend from the rocky area on gradual switchbacks. After a sharp left, cross the creek again, this time on boulders, before returning to the parking area.

Your visit to this falls will be enhanced with a hike to Linville Falls (see page 129), which begins at the same parking area.

DIRECTIONS Leave Linville and head south on US 221 to Pineola. Take NC 181 south about 2 miles, and access the Blue Ridge Parkway on the left. Travel south to milepost 316.4, and turn left onto the 1.4-mile spur road that leads to Linville Falls. Leave from the sidewalk on the right at the lower end of the parking lot, and head slightly up and into the woods.

GPS TRAILHEAD COORDINATES
35.953700, -81.926533

DUGGERS CREEK FALLS

Marion

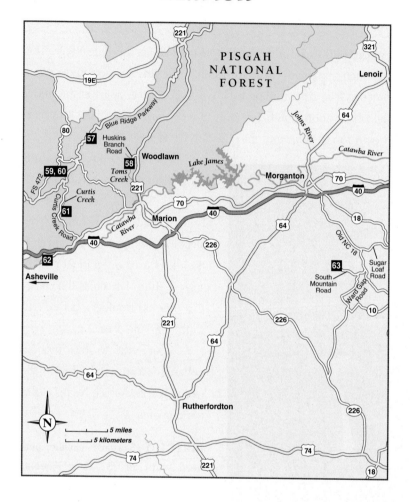

57 CRABTREE FALLS
[2.7-mile loop, moderate]

Crabtree Falls is a Blue Ridge waterfall classic, a must-do hike. The falls plunge 70 feet over a rock face, and you can view them from a hiker bridge over Crabtree Creek. I suggest going in the early morning to avoid the crowd. Additionally, morning is the best time to photograph the cataract; the spiller lies on the west side of the Blue Ridge, so the sun hits the waterfall in the afternoon, creating harsh lighting and shadows.

Before it was part of the Blue Ridge Parkway, Crabtree Creek turned a cornmill during the first half of the 1800s. The Penlands owned the property, and Billy Bradshaw managed it, hiring locals to help with crops, livestock, and, most important, the mill. The cornmill was the main source of income; families came from surrounding valleys to bring their corn to grind. Because the creek

CRABTREE FALLS

had a small but fast current, Bradshaw used a tub mill. This type of mill was designed for mountain streams and turned horizontally instead of vertically.

Crabtree Falls Trail is known for its wildflowers—more than three dozen species—including lady's slippers, wild orchids, and jack-in-the-pulpits. The path leads down gradual switchbacks through an oak–hickory forest. You'll pass through the campground on the way to and from the falls (trail parking is no longer allowed in the campground). Cross several wet-weather springs, where salamanders flourish, before reaching the base of the falls at 1.1 miles. The hikers' bridge across the creek makes for an ideal photography locale.

Cross the creek and begin the 1.6-mile return route, which is not as steep as backtracking. As you climb the moderate switchbacks, you are rewarded with a different view of the falls. Once you reach the ridge, the trail is gentler, crossing the creek and several of its tributaries on bridges. The trail leads through the campground en route back to the Parkway.

DIRECTIONS From Asheville, take the Blue Ridge Parkway north about 43 miles to milepost 338.9 and turn left into the Crabtree Falls Area. Immediately turn left and reach the upper trailhead parking near the former visitor center.

GPS TRAILHEAD COORDINATES 35.812541, -82.143360

58 TOMS CREEK FALLS
[0.8-mile out-and-back, easy]

An excellent all-access trail takes you the short distance to the visually appealing tall cataract. The pea gravel path, designed to accommodate "fat tire" wheelchairs, includes gentle switchbacks that lead to an overlook of the 60-foot multitiered cataract that plunges into a small pool and then fans out, flowing between rocks in shallow braids. Additionally, you can stand on a natural rock viewing promontory from which many a photo has been taken.

Toms Creek Falls also has a bit of history. Two stone bridge pilings remain from a narrow-gauge railroad used in the 1930s to transport timber and people.

The all-access Falls Branch Trail is your conduit for this thrilling spiller. Leave the parking area on the wide gravel track, crossing a tributary of Falls Branch on a bridge at 0.2 mile. Continue up the richly wooded valley, reaching

Toms Creek Falls

an observation deck at the base of Toms Creek Falls; stairs lead closer to the cataract. Here, you gain a face-on view of this tall plunger dancing down a stone face. Remember, this waterfall has a smallish watershed, so it can be a mere trickle in summer and autumn.

DIRECTIONS From the intersection of US 70 and US 211 in Marion, head north on US 221. You will reach the community of Woodlawn after about 7 miles. Turn left on Huskins Branch Road. Go 1.4 miles and park on the right in a gravel lot before a bridge.

GPS TRAILHEAD COORDINATES 35.774664, -82.056763

59 ROARING FORK FALLS

[1.4-mile out-and-back, easy]

Roaring Fork is in the Appalachian District of Pisgah National Forest and eventually flows into the South Toe River. The trailhead is at the entrance to the U.S. Forest Service's Busick Work Center. The hike uses a gated forest road, now a double-track trail. At 0.6 mile, split right, away from the gated forest road, bridging Roaring Fork. Continue upstream of the wooden bridge and at 0.7 mile reach Roaring Fork Falls, which dramatically dances 90 feet down a narrow rockslide. Don't be tempted to scale the sides of this angled cataract; they are quite slippery.

DIRECTIONS From Asheville, drive about 38 miles to milepost 344.1, and exit north onto NC 80. Drive north 2.3 miles, then turn left onto County Road 1205, which becomes Forest Road 472 (there is a sign for FR 472 at the intersection). Take the first left (after 0.1 mile) at the sign indicating Roaring Fork Falls and Busick Work Center. The road ends at the work center. Park near the gate on the right.

GPS TRAILHEAD COORDINATES 35.768482, -82.195268

60 SETROCK CREEK FALLS
[1.0-mile out-and-back, easy]

Setrock Creek Falls is located in Pisgah National Forest at the Black Mountain Recreation Area. In addition to the waterfall hike, you can ride on a bicycle trail; float down the South Toe River in an inner tube; or climb Mount Mitchell, the highest peak in the East, using the 5.6-mile Mount Mitchell Trail.

Black Mountain Campground, at an elevation of 3,000 feet, is open April–October. The tent and trailer sites (no hookups) have tables, fire rings, grills, and lantern posts; the sites are offered on a first-come, first-served basis. Hot showers are available.

From the trailhead parking area, walk across the auto bridge toward Black Mountain Campground, crossing the South Toe River. From here, head left on the forest road toward Briar Bottom Group Camp; then split left again, joining the River Loop, a hiking trail. The South Toe River flows to your left, and the group camp road is on your right. At 0.2 mile, the Mount Mitchell Trail leads right up to the highest point in the East. Continue in bottomlands. Ahead, bridge a tributary, then turn right onto the spur to Setrock Creek Falls. Cross the forest road to Briar Bottom Group Camp and head up the valley of Setrock Creek. At 0.5 mile, come to the base of the 60-foot cataract. Setrock Falls has four distinct levels, each more than 10 feet high. The creek splashes over small boulders and then flows the short distance to the South Toe River. If you want to continue the River Loop, it will lead you back to the trailhead after making a 4.1-mile circuit.

DIRECTIONS From Asheville, take the Blue Ridge Parkway north about 30 miles to milepost 351.9. Turn left on Forest Road 472/South Toe River Road, and follow it 4.4 miles to Black Mountain Campground, on your left. The trailhead is on the right just beyond the left turn into the campground.

GPS TRAILHEAD COORDINATES 35.750952, -82.220233

Setrock Creek Falls

61 HICKORY BRANCH FALLS
[1.2-mile out-and-back, easy]

Hickory Branch Falls is accessed from Curtis Creek Campground. Despite being in the shadow of the Blue Ridge Parkway, the falls and campground are most often reached from I-40 near Old Fort. Hickory Branch tumbles through a deep vale hemmed in by Buckeye Knob and Moses Ridge. During its frothy flow through crowded rhododendron thickets and rising hardwoods, Hickory Branch finds an erosion-resistant cliff, spilling into a gravelly pool ensconced in vegetation.

The Hickory Branch Trail begins in the upper part of the campground, near campsite 16C, located on the right after a bridge takes you over to the right bank of Curtis Creek. A trail sign indicates the path's beginning, backed against a hill. The trail immediately switchbacks over the hill, dropping into the Hickory Branch drainage. At 0.1 mile, a rock hop takes you to the right bank of Hickory Branch, where the trail meanders upstream. Doghobble, rhododendron, and holly crowd the path. At 0.3 mile, rock-hop over to the left bank of the clear mountain rill. The hollow closes in. Pass some warm-up cascades at 0.4 mile, and then climb away from the stream. Reach a small man-made flat, likely constructed when this vale was logged. Otherwise, there is nary a level site in this hollow. As you continue up the valley, Hickory Branch Falls sonorously announces its presence. The trail takes you to the top of the falls at 0.6 mile. Gaze down as the stream spills over a 20-foot rock face. Rhododendron and doghobble frame the pour-over. A scramble trail just before the top of the falls leads you to the base, where a shallow, gravelly pool briefly stills the water before it presses on to feed Curtis Creek.

Enhance a trip to the falls by adding other recreation opportunities at Curtis Creek. The campground stretches along its tumbling namesake stream. The primary camping area has been revamped with a paved loop and graveled sites, each with a picnic table, fire ring, lantern post, and tent pad. More primitive, well-dispersed sites are located below the primary camping area. The upper camping area, where the hike to Hickory Branch Falls starts, presents grassy, open sites. The campground is generally open mid-April–December. A monument to the Civilian Conservation Corps is located in the upper campground on the left. These workers built trails and roads around this area during the Great Depression.

HICKORY BRANCH FALLS

Take note: If the campground is closed, you will have to park at the gate on the lower end of Curtis Creek Campground, adding 0.6 mile more each way, making this a 2.4-mile hike round-trip.

Trout fishing is a regular pastime at Curtis Creek during the warmer months. Swimmers can jump in the creek at some of the deeper pools, and hikers may want to consider a cool dip. In addition to the Hickory Branch Trail, hikers can take the Lead Mine Gap Trail and make a 7-mile or so loop if they don't mind closing the circle by walking down Curtis Creek Road/Forest Road 482. Be apprised, the Lead Mine Gap Trail may be overgrown. The better-maintained Snooks Nose Trail starts below the campground. It ascends 2 miles, eased by switchbacks aplenty, to a rock outcrop with vistas; it then travels onward 2 more miles to the Blue Ridge Parkway and the tower atop Green Knob. The full 4-mile hike gains 2,800 feet.

You can also access Hickory Branch Falls and Curtis Creek Campground from milepost 347.5 on the Blue Ridge Parkway via FR 482. However, both the upper forest road and the Parkway may be closed in winter, so we suggest coming from the lower end during the cold, inclement season. However, during summer you could take a spin on the Parkway.

DIRECTIONS From Exit 72 on I-40 about 20 miles east of Asheville, take Main Street/US 70 east through Old Fort. At 2.6 miles, turn left on Curtis Creek Road. Follow the paved road as it turns to gravel and reaches a gate at 4.6 miles. You will have to park here when the campground is closed; otherwise, proceed up the forest road to reach the campground after 5.2 miles. Park in the creekside spots near the upper part of the campground, above the paved loop.

GPS TRAILHEAD COORDINATES 35.690850, -82.196467

62 CATAWBA FALLS

[2.4-mile out-and-back, moderate]

For a long time, access to Catawba Falls was an issue, but now it has been resolved, and this time for good. Owned by the Pisgah National Forest since 1989, the falls could not be legally accessed because they were encircled by private property. Then the Foothills Conservancy acquired a critical tract connecting to the falls and transferred it over to the Pisgah National Forest. Now we can hike to the falls in complete confidence.

The trail to Catawba Falls has been a popular hike for a century and a half. You follow the Catawba River the whole way. It is fascinating to watch it change from a flat, quiet stream to a narrow mountain creek filled with small rapids and drops. At 0.2 mile, cross the river. If the Catawba is up, expect to get your feet wet. At 0.8 mile you will cross Clover Patch Branch just above a slender 6-foot chute. At 0.9 mile, a spur drops left to a two-tiered, 18-foot waterfall below an old dam. At 1.1 miles, hop Chestnut Branch as the Catawba valley narrows. At 1.2 miles, come to the base of the multistage, 100-foot cataract falling in multiple

LOWER CATAWBA FALLS

forms. Catawba Falls is only a few miles from the river's headwaters, which lie on the ridge to the west—the county line between McDowell and Buncombe—that forms the Eastern Continental Divide.

History buffs will be interested in the sawmill site and old dam site that you can see en route to the main falls. In 1924 Colonel Daniel Adams built the dam as well as two powerhouses. With the help of the Catawba River, he supplied Old Fort with its first electric lights. During the last few years the Adams family owned the land, they built the sawmill so they could sell lumber to pay the taxes on the land.

DIRECTIONS From Exit 73 on I-40 near Old Fort, join Catawba River Road and follow it west 3.2 miles to dead-end at the trailhead.

GPS TRAILHEAD COORDINATES 35.613699, -82.230554

63 HIGH SHOALS FALLS AND UPPER FALLS
[2.7-mile loop, moderate]

High Shoals Falls, on Jacob's Fork River, may well be the most spectacular geological feature in South Mountains State Park. Not only is the waterfall fantastic, but so are the extensive boardwalk and steps that lead to the observation deck at its base.

Take the High Shoals Falls Loop Trail. At 0.4 mile, reach Shinny Creek Picnic Area and stay left. A large volume and variety of wildflowers color this trail in the spring. Hike a half mile along Jacob's Fork before reaching the base of High Shoals Falls. The maze of well-designed wooden bridges allows passage across the boulder-strewn creek and up a steep ravine on more than 200 steps. At the viewpoint, about 20 feet from the falls, you can feel the spray from the river as it gushes over a ledge from the top of an 80-foot rock cliff, forming this gorgeous, narrow waterfall.

The trail continues up steps and across a small footbridge, where you can view Upper Falls, a two-tiered, 20-foot pour-over spilling scenic in its own right, complete with a picturesque hikers' bridge. Many years back, you had to hike a separate trail to see Upper Falls, but the park linked two trails to form High Shoals Falls Loop Trail. The connector climbs around the rock cliff and crosses at the top of Upper Falls.

High Shoals Falls

An early area settler named Dave Bibby milled corn at the top of High Shoals Falls near the cascades of Upper Falls. He also lived close to the river. It is possible that Jacob's Fork River was named after Jacob Bibby, a relative of Dave's.

The trail continues and loops back to Jacob's Fork Picnic Area. You will depart the creek and travel through an oak–hickory forest as you leave the ridge. Gradually descend back to Shinny Creek Picnic Area and on to the trailhead using the Hemlock Nature Trail. The gentle path is chock-full of interpretive information. At one time, the area that is now South Mountains State Park was known for producing moonshine. In the park, several dismantled stills are marked by rusted buckets and axed barrels. The name Shinny Creek was derived from the moonshining days.

Jacob's Fork River was one of the first rivers in North Carolina to be considered an outstanding water resource. The watershed is extremely pure because the river's headwaters are contained within park boundaries. Three major creeks—Murray Branch, Nettles Branch, and Jacob's Fork Branch—form the upper river.

DIRECTIONS From Exit 118 on I-40, about 4 miles west of Hickory, take Old NC Highway 10 south 1.1 miles, then keep straight, joining Shoupes Grove Church Road. In 0.8 mile turn left onto Miller Bridge Road. In 5.3 miles turn left onto NC 18 South. In 2.0 miles turn acutely right onto Sugar Loaf Road. In 4.2 miles turn left onto Old NC 18. In 2.7 miles turn right onto Ward Gap Road. Follow Ward Gap Road 1.4 miles to enter South Mountains State Park. After 3.3 miles, dead-end at the High Shoals Falls parking area.

GPS TRAILHEAD COORDINATES 35.602805, -81.627909

Asheville

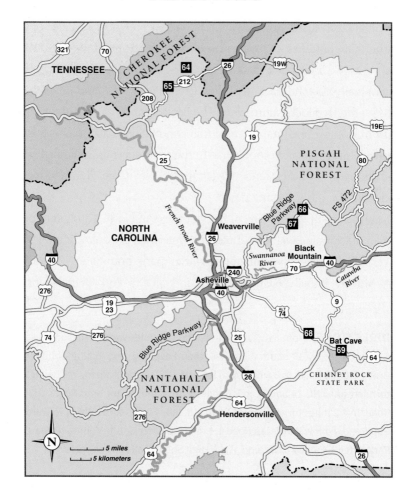

64 WHITEOAK FLATS BRANCH CASCADE
[1.8-mile round-trip, easy]

This rewarding waterfall hike is set in the remote Shelton Laurel Backcountry of the Pisgah National Forest. It makes an eye-catching long, white slide that will leave you wondering why more people don't seek it. Note the trailhead memorial to Jerry Miller, a Carolinian and advocate of national forests. By way of the Supreme Court, he forced federal law enforcement to patrol national forests rather than leaving them in the hands of often undermanned local authorities. Bridge Big Creek on the Jerry Miller Trail, heading downstream. This flat will fill with wildflowers in spring, including white trillium by the thousands. Surmount a ridge dividing Big Creek from Whiteoak Flats Branch, avoiding an old route that crossed private property. Turn into Whiteoak Flats Branch watershed at 0.3 mile and head up the steep-sided valley among rhododendron, sourwood, pine, and magnolia.

The valley of Whiteoak Flats Branch closes in at 0.9 mile. Here, a long slide pours 80 feet down the hollow, widening at its base, then drops in stages before slowing. Winter's barren trees reveal the full fall. This cataract is so seldom visited there is but a faint path to its base.

DIRECTIONS From Hot Springs, take US 25 South/US 70 East 5.1 miles and turn left on NC 208 North. In 3.5 miles turn right on NC 212 North and follow it 11.0 miles to turn left on Big Creek Road, near Carmen Church of God. Follow Big Creek Road 1.2 miles. The road seems to end near a barn. Here, angle left onto Forest Road 111, taking the gravel road over a small creek. Enter Pisgah National Forest. At 0.4 mile beyond the barn, veer left onto a short spur road to dead-end at Jerry Miller trailhead.

GPS TRAILHEAD COORDINATES 36.023317, -82.652667

65 HICKEY FORK FALLS
[2.6-mile round-trip, moderate]

This is another undervisited waterfall in the Shelton Laurel Backcountry. You will likely experience these rewarding cataracts by yourself. From the parking area, walk up Forest Road 465, passing around a metal gate. Just ahead, the Hickey Fork Trail leaves left, immediately crossing East Prong Hickey Fork on a cool log bridge with handrails. After spanning East Prong, the slender path heads upstream through rhododendron before turning away from the creek at 0.1 mile. Work around a low ridge, then join a tributary of West Prong Hickey Fork. Reach and rock-hop West Prong Hickey Fork at 0.5 mile. Head upstream on a slender single-track in lush forest under which lie doghobble, ferns, and an ocean of rhododendron. Trickling branches cross over the trail, adding volume to West Prong Hickey Fork. Ascend the narrowing valley and come to Hickey Fork Cascade at 1.1 miles. This long, sloping cataract flows over a smooth rock bed, dropping in excess of 100 feet. Be careful here: a slide down this wild waterfall would not end well.

Above, the stream falls in pools and drops. Come to the classic curtain-type Hickey Fork Falls at 1.3 miles. It starts sloped but then dives over a wide rock ledge during its 35-foot descent into a crystalline plunge pool. The fact that there is but a scant path to the base of this impressive pour-over testifies to the under-visitation of this secluded spiller.

DIRECTIONS From Hot Springs, take US 25 South/US 70 East 5.1 miles, then turn left on NC 208 North. In 3.5 miles turn right on NC 212 North and follow it 6.9 miles to turn left on Hickey Fork Road, which becomes FR 465 upon entering Pisgah National Forest. Follow Hickey Fork Road 1.1 miles to a seasonally closed gate and parking area on your right.

GPS TRAILHEAD COORDINATES 35.994528, -82.704611

66 GLASSMINE FALLS
[mileage and difficulty not applicable]

From a pulloff on the Blue Ridge Parkway (at 5,197 feet), you can look across the valley and see Glassmine Falls sliding 800 feet down Horse Range Ridge. Surprised at the height? It is hard to judge how tall a waterfall is when it is so far away.

Glassmine Falls is part of the Asheville watershed. Rivers and creeks run down the slopes of this valley into the North Fork Reservoir, and the water is pumped to the city. So Glassmine Falls plays a part in supplying water to the people in Asheville.

Near the base of the falls are an early-1900s pit mine and cabin site. Miners once used pack animals to haul mica to Micaville and Burnsville in the Toe

River Valley. It is the oldest mineral industry in the area, and a truckload of high-quality mica could bring in thousands of dollars then. Mica used to be referred to as isinglass, and people in the mountains called it glass, which is how the waterfall got its name.

This is a wet-weather falls, which means it will almost disappear during periods of low water. If you cannot view Glassmine Falls after a heavy rain, try late afternoon. With the sun shining on the falls, the wet rock face reflects like glass.

An observation area with a wooden bench—up the paved sidewalk and to the left—makes a nice rest stop. In addition to the view east of Glassmine Falls, look west for an incredible view of Roan Mountain. Binoculars and a camera lens with a focal length of at least 200 millimeters will make this waterfall more rewarding.

DIRECTIONS Pick up the Blue Ridge Parkway in Asheville and head north about 25 miles. Turn into the overlook for Glassmine Falls on the right at milepost 361.2.

GPS TRAILHEAD COORDINATES 35.734800, -82.344200

67 DOUGLAS FALLS AND CASCADE FALLS
[6.6-mile out-and-back, strenuous]

This waterfall trek starts near Craggy Gardens, a Blue Ridge Parkway recreation area famous for its balds that support wildflowers, grasses, and shrubs, such as rhododendron, mountain laurel, and flame azalea. Don't miss seeing the balds between mid-June and early July when the pink and purple blooms of the native rhododendron star in the most dazzling flower pageant on the Parkway, coloring the slopes and peaks of the Craggy Mountains. Spring is also an ideal time to hike to Douglas Falls: the waterfalls are robust, while wildflowers big and small color the highlands. Consider sturdy shoes for the rocky hike.

Join the mile-high Mountains-to-Sea Trail northbound, bordered by storm-stunted hardwoods, and pass below Craggy Gardens Visitor Center. Head out Big Fork Ridge amid gray boulders and green grasses shaded by beech trees. Dip into the Carter Creek watershed, of which Waterfall Creek is a tributary. At 1.0 mile, leave left on the Douglas Falls Trail, Forest Trail #162. The slender path slithers downhill in frequent switchbacks. At 1.6 miles, step over a small unnamed stream. The watercourse has an unnamed 25-foot slide cascade above the crossing, but that isn't Cascade Falls.

Reach Cascade Falls at 1.9 miles. You stand in the middle of a hard-to-believe long rock cascade. The cataract starts well above the trail crossing and alternately pours and dives over multiple layers of rock, shooting across the path, then somersaulting over more rock into crowding brush, then out of view. The cataract extends beyond sight in both directions, making it impossible to see the whole thing. At the trail crossing, note the metal poles embedded in the rock. A cable connected to the embedded poles once ran across the slick rock slab you must traverse. The crossing can be unnerving—a slip would have

DOUGLAS FALLS   *photo: Nicole Blouin*

you sliding down Cascade Falls. However, at normal flows you won't even wet your boot tops. Old-growth hemlocks once shaded the stream and trail ahead but were decimated by the hemlock woolly adelgid.

Lose elevation, now in oaks. Cross another stream at 2.2 miles, and come to another tributary at 2.6 miles. This unnamed creek soon creates Douglas Falls. At 3.0 miles, the path makes a hard switchback left. Ahead, come to a house-size boulder. The Douglas Falls Trail descends left around it. You can hear the falls. Trails go left and right; stay right with the official path to the falls rather than taking the erosive user-created track that splits left.

Reach Douglas Falls at 3.3 miles. Here, the unnamed stream plunges from a bare cliff into a curved, overhanging stone showground framed in trees. You can make a misty walk behind the slender spiller, soaking in the descending stream from front and back. There may be more hikers at the falls than you expected, as most will have come the easier, albeit less scenic, way from Forest Road 74.

DIRECTIONS From Asheville, take the Blue Ridge Parkway northbound 18 miles to the Craggy Gardens Visitor Center, on your left at milepost 364.6. Do not go to the Craggy Gardens Picnic Area, south of the visitor center. Pick up the Mountains-to-Sea Trail on the southwest corner of the paved parking area.

GPS TRAILHEAD COORDINATES 35.699400, -82.379983

68 FALLS OF FLORENCE NATURE PRESERVE
[2.2-mile round-trip, easy]

In the upper Hickory Nut Creek valley, a man named Tom Florence bought a 600-acre retreat along the south slope of Little Pisgah Mountain. Later, he donated the land to the Nature Conservancy. They in turn developed a trail system, part of which accesses a pair of cascades that exhibit dissimilar characteristics despite being on the same creek. First you will see the stream make a two-tiered, 15-foot descent into a plunge pool, while the second cascade froths white for 60 feet down a fingerlike chute, losing 30 feet of elevation in the process.

From the Florence Nature Preserve trailhead, marked by a stone chimney, join a yellow-blazed singletrack trail north, switchbacking up intriguingly named Burntshirt Mountain. Come along a rocked-in spring below the trail before a stone slab bridge takes you over a little branch at 0.4 mile. Come along

WATERFALL AT FLORENCE NATURE PRESERVE

the unnamed stream where the waterfalls are found. At 0.9 mile, cross that creek to reach the Blue Trail. Turn left here, heading downhill and downstream where at 1.0 mile you come to the first waterfall, the two-tiered 15-footer, viewed from a hikers' bridge crossing the creek. Continue downstream, bridging the creek yet again to reach the spur trail leading to the slender chute fall. The spur quickly takes you to the faucet-style cataract, sliding down a slim channel, demonstrating that waterfalls of the Blue Ridge come in all shapes and sizes.

DIRECTIONS From downtown Asheville, take I-240 east to Exit 9 (Blue Ridge Parkway/Bat Cave), joining US 74A. Take US 74A east 13.8 miles to the trailhead on your left, 0.9 mile beyond the Upper Hickory Nut Gorge Community Center. Parking area is limited.

GPS TRAILHEAD COORDINATES 35.473333, -82.332111

69 HICKORY NUT FALLS

- **Top** [1.5-mile out-and-back, strenuous]
- **Bottom** [1.4-mile out-and-back, moderate]

Ride an elevator up 26 stories through solid granite and cross a clear-span bridge onto the famous monolith of Chimney Rock to start your hike to Hickory Nut

Falls—a most interesting way to reach the trailhead. The project required 18 months and 8 tons of dynamite to complete in 1949. The elevator was completely redone in 2012, but the kinks weren't fully worked out until 2018. This is just one way to access the waterfall at Chimney Rock State Park, formerly a private operation, where Fall Creek flows over a vertical lip on Chimney Rock Mountain, dropping an impressive 404 feet. The elevator operator will introduce the area to you on your ride up. Several scenes from the 1992 film version of *The Last of the Mohicans* were shot at the park, including the climactic fight scene at the top of the falls.

Chimney Rock is located on the eastern edge of the Blue Ridge Mountains, about 20 miles southeast of Asheville. Get a park map when you arrive and decide how to spend your day. The Hickory Nut Falls Trail will take you to the base of the 404-foot cataract. Stand at the bottom of the falls and feel the mist drifting onto you as you admire the white froth and the cliffs that rise around it. It is a 1.5-mile round-trip. The Exclamation Point Trail leads to superlative views of the Hickory Nut Creek Gorge, as well as the Opera Box, Devils Head, and Exclamation Point itself, replete with awe-inspiring panoramas. The Skyline Trail continues 0.7 mile beyond Exclamation Point to the top of Hickory Nut Falls. Still other paths explore park highlights that complement the falls.

Hickory Nut Falls aside, the 1,000-acre park is worth a visit for other reasons: astonishing views, well-designed interpretive trails, and an informative nature center. From the top of towering Chimney Rock, you can see the Broad River cutting its way through Hickory Nut Gorge, Lake Lure below, and Kings Mountain, 75 miles away. The trails have numbered stations and accompanying interpretive pamphlets to enhance your experience. At the nature center, you can learn about the birds, wildflowers, and geology of the park.

DIRECTIONS From Asheville, head east on US 74A, which becomes US 64/74 after Bat Cave. You can pick up US 74A from the east side of the city at the junction of I-240 and I-40, at Exit 9 or 53, respectively. Chimney Rock State Park is on the right after about 20 miles. Check the park's website (chimneyrockpark.com) for seasonal opening and closing times, as well as rates and other information.

GPS TRAILHEAD COORDINATES 35.439781, -82.248597

Brevard

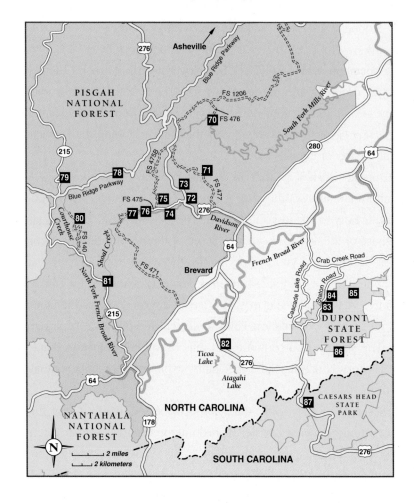

70 HIGH FALLS

[4.2-mile out-and-back, moderate–strenuous]

High Falls is not high. Nor is it particularly wide, or powerful, or distinctive, or easy to access. But of all the things 18-foot High Falls is not, the most important virtue is that it's not frequently visited.

The South Mills River is a long and beautiful stream of many incarnations. Flowing off the east side of the Blue Ridge in the Pisgah National Forest, the river gathers numerous highland tributaries, including those flowing through the famed Pink Beds, and begins its 3,000-foot descent from the Blue Ridge down to its convergence with the North Mills River. At an altitude of over 3,200 feet, the Pink Beds are an unusual highland bog. Part of the historic 6,500-acre Cradle of Forestry tract of the Pisgah National Forest, the Pink Beds may have received their name from the startling array of rosebay rhododendrons, mountain laurels, wild azaleas, and great masses of wild pink phlox—a botanist's paradise. Another source of the name could have been the pink rock that was once mined in the area. Name aside, High Falls is worth a visit, and so are the Pink Beds.

High Falls is the most notable of many cataracts along this stream cutting an ultrascenic valley. Trails extend along the South Mills River nearly the entire portion of its journey through the forested lands of Pisgah. Many gristmills and sawmills once graced the streams and rivers of these mountains, so it would be easy to conclude this was the origin for the name South Mills River. Actually, Revolutionary War veteran Major William Mills named the river after himself. In 1787 he was awarded 640 acres in return for his military service.

The trek to the falls begins at the Wolf Ford primitive camping area, near an old stone USGS water-gauging station. Hike around the pole gate at the end of Forest Road 476, continuing on the now-overgrown balance of the logging road, sharing the trail with mountain bikers. The translucent South Mills River flows but 20 feet wide here over boulders and beside outcrops, framed in evergreens, sans the decimated hemlock. A small, unnamed stream adds its flow at the Otter Hole, a popular summertime swimming locale, reached at 0.7 mile. Rock protrusions and sandy borders fashion spots for swimmers to bask in the heat following a chilly summertime dip.

The trail is easy, wide, and well used. At 1.0 mile, you reach an intersection. Here, the official South Mills River Trail heads right across the river on a former road bridge, but for now, head left up Billy Branch 0.1 mile, then descend to the base of Billy Branch Falls, a 22-foot, angled cascade dancing down a rhododendron-bordered rock face. Don't pass this pour-over in your eagerness to reach High Falls.

Return to the bridge. From here, do not follow the official South Mills River Trail away from the water; rather, continue along the north (left) bank of the Mills River on a user-maintained, formerly official trail, aiming for High Falls. The mountain bikers have been left behind as the much narrower pathway climbs well above South Fork Mills River, shortcutting a big bend in the river. Descend to reach the ford of the Mills River at 1.9 miles. Expect to get your feet wet here. In cold times I have simply taken off my shoes and socks, waded across with trekking poles, and then put my shoes back on. Pass a slide cascade before coming to unmistakable High Falls at 2.1 miles. You can walk to the top of the falls, but keep going and find the spur trail leading to the outsize plunge pool at the base of the cataract. It can be argued that the pool is equally impressive as 18-foot High Falls itself, as the waterfall charges over an irregular rock face, flowing in varied forms, depending on water levels.

DIRECTIONS From the intersection of US 64 and US 276 in the town of Pisgah Forest, travel 11.7 miles north on US 276. Go right on Forest Road 1206 (Yellow Gap Road) and follow the gravel road 3.3 miles. Go right again on FR 476 (South Mills River Road) and travel 1.3 miles to the end of the road. The trailhead leaves from the lower end of the parking area.

GPS TRAILHEAD COORDINATES 35.366459, -82.739075

71 TWIN FALLS AND AVERY CREEK FALLS
[4.0-mile out-and-back, easy–moderate]

Everyone likes buy-one-get-one-free specials at the grocery store because you get double the goods for the same price. This is also true for Twin Falls; plus, you get Avery Creek Falls as a bonus. On this hike, you get two distinct waterfalls for your efforts, and like fraternal twins, each has its own special characteristics. How

AVERY CREEK FALLS

about throwing in a bonus waterfall, Avery Branch Falls, that you can see along the way? That amounts to a deal and a half! Avery Creek Falls is a wider-than-tall cataract with a fine plunge pool that will be a warm-up waterfall for you.

The first waterfall of the Twin Falls, fed by Henry Branch, is an 80-foot cascade. The trail crosses at the base of the waterfall, giving you an excellent view as the moderate volume leaps over the edge high above. The water splashes its way down ledges, but rocks in the creek at the base allow you to stay dry if you are photographing the scene. The second waterfall, on an unnamed tributary of Henry Branch, is just 30 yards from the first. The low-volume drift from this fall is light and airy, trailing down 100 feet.

The watershed for the Twin Falls is smallish, so I recommend winter-spring for a visit, especially since hikers' bridges enable dry-footed passage year-round. Start on the Buckhorn Gap Trail as it traces an old forest road above Avery Creek. At 0.6 mile, reach Avery Creek Falls. The cataract is usually accessed from the Avery Creek Trail, on the other side of Avery Creek. Nevertheless, a scramble trail descends to the 10-foot-high, wide falls with an alluring plunge pool bordered by a gravel bar.

Beyond the falls you will meet the Avery Creek Trail, with Buckhorn Gap Trail and Avery Creek Trail running in conjunction before splitting 0.1 mile distant. At this point, remain with the Buckhorn Gap Trail to cross Avery Creek right on a hikers' bridge, while the Avery Creek Trail heads left. The Buckhorn Gap Trail now turns up Henry Creek, a tributary of Avery Creek. Ahead, frequent hikers' bridges span the creek while equestrians ford the stream (I've never seen a horse on this trail). At 1.7 miles, head left, joining the Twin Falls Trail; the Buckhorn Gap Trail stays straight. You'll span Henry Branch, heading deeper into a high-walled vale. At 2.0 miles, you enter the steep mountain cathedral where Henry Branch and its tributary form the Twin Falls, tumbling side by side to merge at their bases in a cavalcade of cascading aqua. The fall to the left on Henry Branch is more picturesque as it spills in four widening steps. It also has more volume. The fall on the right is higher but more difficult to see due to heavy growth along the long, tumbling cata-ract, though you can hike along and up

TWIN FALLS

this fall to a veil-like ledge drop where it starts.

DIRECTIONS From the intersection of NC 280 and US 276 in the town of Pisgah Forest, take US 276 north for 2.1 miles, then turn right on Forest Road 477. You will see a sign here directing you toward Pisgah Riding Stables. Follow FR 477 for 2.5 miles; the trailhead will be on your right, 0.8 mile beyond the Pisgah Riding Stables. Trailhead parking is limited.

GPS TRAILHEAD COORDINATES 35.316417, -82.752817

72 LOOKING GLASS FALLS
[mileage and difficulty not applicable]

Does the classic waterfall exist? Most people agree that Looking Glass Falls is the epitome of a postcard waterfall. Because of its easy access, Looking Glass Falls is a major tourist attraction, one of the most well-known falls in the eastern United States.

LOOKING GLASS FALLS

This waterfall is a symbol of Pisgah National Forest. The image shows up in national-forest and local tourism literature, on the Internet, and on area souvenirs. And, yes, you can still get a postcard showing this definitive waterfall.

Holding rainwater like a sponge, the forest cover atop Looking Glass Rock gives rise to the creeks that feed the falls. The high volume from Looking Glass Creek creates a 30-foot-wide, undivided rush of water that surges over a 65-foot sheer drop. As the waters dive into the pool at the base, a misty spray drifts upward to coat the sides of the towering granite shelf.

Looking Glass Creek eventually flows into the Davidson River, which south of Avery Creek is stocked from the nearby fish hatchery. In the early spring, you will find the streams busy with anglers trying their luck for brook, brown, and rainbow trout. The hatchery raises and stocks thousands of trout in the streams of the Pisgah National Forest each year.

Many present-day highways in the Pisgah National Forest follow old railroad beds. US 276, the road past the falls, follows almost the exact location of an old railroad bed that transported timber out of the forest to the mills. In the early 1920s, the Carr Lumber Company built and maintained 75 miles of railroad in what is now the Pisgah National Forest.

For 30 years, lumber was one of the most thriving industries in Transylvania County. It was not uncommon to see 3–4 million board feet of lumber stacked around the Pisgah Forest Mill. The double-band mill was capable of sawing up to 100,000 board feet a day. Nowadays, ecotourism has replaced the extractive era of a century ago.

DIRECTIONS From the intersection of US 64 and NC 280 on the northeast side of Brevard, take US 276 north 5.7 miles. The parking area is on the right. You can observe the falls from your car or walk the steps to the base of the falls.

GPS TRAILHEAD COORDINATES 35.296347, -82.769551

73 MOORE COVE FALLS
[1.2-mile out-and-back, easy]

Moore Cove Falls could be an all-day trip—not because it's a long hike, but because it's such a serene and restful place that you could easily lose track of time. The gentle waters of Moore Creek dribble over a small series of stairstep ledges and then rain down 50 feet over a sheer drop to the creek below. The trail goes behind the docile curtain into a large granite cove. You can sit and look through the falling water without getting wet. It's like watching a summer rain through a window. The cool nook provides plenty of seating and could easily accommodate a group of friends.

The falls were named for Adam Q. Moore, a onetime US commissioner and justice of the peace. Moore owned 50 acres along Looking Glass Creek. Although he owned the land for only three years, his name became permanently attached to the creek and the falls. He sold his entire parcel in 1880 to the King family, who transferred ownership to the Vanderbilt estate in 1901 for the modest sum of $155.

The waterfall hike begins by bridging Looking Glass Creek on a pedestrian span, then follows Looking Glass Creek downstream before turning up Moore Creek and into Moore Cove on a well graded path. The trail ends after 0.6 mile at a wooden observation platform, yet visitors still go closer to—and behind—the 50-foot veil-like cataract. The hike to Moore Cove Falls is very popular due to its proximity to Looking Glass Falls.

DIRECTIONS From the intersection of US 64 and NC 280 on the northeast side of Brevard, take US 276 north 6.7 miles to the trailhead parking on the right-hand side of US 276. Moore Cove Falls is 1 mile up the road from Looking Glass Falls.

GPS TRAILHEAD COORDINATES 35.305618, -82.774597

74 CEDAR ROCK CREEK FALLS
[2.0-mile round-trip, moderate]

This waterfall adventure is often hiked as a 5.8-mile loop and includes a visit to not only tumbling Cedar Rock Cascades but also John Rock, an open stone promontory allowing views of nearby Looking Glass Rock as well as the crest of the Blue Ridge. However, the hike to the falls alone is worthy. It starts at the informative Pisgah Center for Wildlife Education deep in the Davidson River valley.

From the rear of the education center, find Forest Road 475C, south of the building. Pass around a pole gate to bridge Cedar Rock Creek, then leave right from the gravel road, joining the Cat Gap Loop hiking trail. Gently ascend,

Cascade of Cedar Rock Creek Falls

roughly paralleling Cedar Rock Creek, and pass fences of the adjacent fish hatchery. At 0.4 mile, bridge Cedar Rock Creek, continuing up the right bank of the stream. The trail pulls back from the waterway before returning at 0.9 mile. Here, an unsigned spur leads down through a sloped campsite to the two primary cataracts that comprise Cedar Rock Creek Falls, an aggregation of cascades. The two main falls drop 15–20 feet each, one diving from a sheer ledge and the other spilling over rounded stone. Exercise caution on these slick paths to the falls. Maps are available at the wildlife center should you want to make John Rock; the panoramas of the fish hatchery below and the surrounding Carolina mountains can be stunning year-round.

DIRECTIONS From the intersection of NC 280 and US 276 on the northeast side of Brevard, take US 276 north 5.2 miles, then turn left on FR 475 toward the Pisgah Center for Wildlife Education. Follow FR 475 for 1.4 miles, then turn left across the bridge over the Davidson River to the wildlife center and fish hatchery. The hike starts behind the wildlife center.

GPS TRAILHEAD COORDINATES 35.284000, -82.791917

75 SLICK ROCK FALLS

[mileage and difficulty not applicable]

Overshadowed by a plethora of spectacular cataracts, Slick Rock Falls is often bypassed, despite being labeled a waterfall on official U.S. Geological Survey topographic maps (many of the falls in this guide are not).

Fed by a wet-weather stream pulsing down the west side of Looking Glass Rock, the waterfall is just a dripping, slick rock during late summer and fall or droughts. However, from late winter through spring, and after thunderstorms, the curtain-type drop is well worth a look. What's more, you can scramble behind the cascade to visit a rock house.

Rock climbers, who use the Slick Rock Falls Trail to reach a climbing spot on Looking Glass Rock, frequent the area. A dispersed camping area is located below the trailhead parking. Though you can see the falls from Forest Road 475B, the Slick Rock Falls Trail affords a closer look. Leave from a trailhead kiosk, mostly containing information for rock climbers. The slender ribbon of a path weaves uphill and then quickly splits. Take the spur going right to the falls. Reach Slick Rock Falls just a few hundred feet from the parking area.

The trail view brings you to the left side of Slick Rock Falls. Here, the unnamed creek cascades about 20 feet over a wide rock face, in a paper-thin, bridal veil–type fashion. Depending on flow levels, the waterfall is nearly as wide as it is long. Below, the stream narrows and gathers, pouring through

SLICK ROCK FALLS

a rock jumble, under the forest road via a culvert, and then through the dispersed camping area to meet its mother stream, Rockhouse Creek.

As you draw closer to Slick Rock Falls, its rock house comes into view. The overhang is largest on the far side of the falls. You can either squeeze behind the flowing water or circle below it to reach the rock house. The cavern adds perspective to Slick Rock Falls, a behind-the-spill viewpoint.

DIRECTIONS From the intersection of NC 280 and US 276 on the northeast side of Brevard, take US 276 north 5.2 miles; then turn left on FR 475 toward the Pisgah Center for Wildlife Education. Follow paved FR 475 for 1.5 miles to FR 475B, on your right just after the left turn into the Pisgah Center. Follow FR 475B for 1.1 miles to reach the parking area and falls on your right.

GPS TRAILHEAD COORDINATES 35.293200, -82.797850

76 COVE CREEK FALLS
[2.2-mile out-and-back, easy]

Cove Creek Falls lies within the waterfall-rich upper Davidson River Valley. A visit is a must for campers staying at Cove Creek Group Camp, located in the flats

COVE CREEK FALLS

below the falls. Draining the south side of the Blue Ridge, Cove Creek picks up tributaries starting nearly a mile high, then gathers momentum to its climactic drop. Combine Cove Creek's flow with a resistant stone outcrop and you find an impressive long and wide cascade. The hike is just right—long enough to get a little exercise but not so long as to become work.

The waterfall walk starts at the gated Forest Road 809, which leads to Cove Creek Group Camp. Walk around the pole gate. It isn't long before the road fords Cove Creek. Fortunately for hikers, a footbridge spans the stream and allows good views of the feisty mountain rill. Rows of rhododendron rise from the creek. Continue up FR 809. Rise to find a long slide cascade on your right at 0.3 mile. A spur trail leads to its base. The slope is such that the cataract is more slide than fall, but it's impressive nonetheless.

At 0.4 mile, leave left from the forest road on the Caney Bottom Trail. The lower end of the group camp, set in a clearing, is just ahead. The singletrack Caney Bottom Trail enters mountain laurel and swings around the left side of the group camp, passing just above the picnic tables as it curves up the valley. Please be courteous if the camp is occupied. The trail rises on the ridge slope above Cove Creek, bordered by oaks and mountain laurels. At 0.7 mile, come to an intersection. Here, you join the Cove Creek Trail as it stays left, while the Caney Bottom Trail drops right. Continue circling around a cove. In winter, Cove Creek Falls is visible through the trees.

At 1.1 miles, a signed spur trail leads to the top of 60-foot Cove Creek Falls. Be careful; the path descends sharply, emerging at the lip of the falls. Views here are limited; however, user-created trails work down to the base of the drop. As you find a rock perch, enjoy your view of Cove Creek Falls as it quickly widens, spilling over a steep rock slope. The water then crashes into less-vertical creased stone, creating multiple pathways for the white froth to descend. The cataract ends in a shallow pool bordered with ample viewing rocks. Note the rock overhang near the falls' base. A few visitors have sought cover beneath it during summer storms. User-created trails continue downstream, linking to the group camp.

DIRECTIONS From the intersection of NC 280 and US 276 on the northeast side of Brevard, take US 276 north 5.2 miles, then turn left on paved FR 475 toward the Pisgah Center for Wildlife Education. Follow FR 475 for 3.0 miles to the Cove Creek Group Camp entrance on your right. Parking is on the left.

GPS TRAILHEAD COORDINATES 35.283150, -82.816967

77 TOMS SPRING FALLS
[0.8-mile out-and-back, easy]

Toms Spring Falls does not appear on official topographic maps because it was only publicized some 50 years ago. Few knew the falls existed until the early 1970s, when Ray Jackson cut the logging road to access the timber management area south of Laurel Ridge. His coworkers started calling this waterfall Jackson Falls, and the name stuck for a while. These days the name Jackson Falls is falling out of favor and the falls are now better known as Toms Spring Falls, after a prospector from this area in the late 19th century. You may also hear it called Daniel Ridge Falls.

Name aside, Toms Spring Falls begins its near-vertical descent down the mountainside 100 feet above the logging road. It cascades, slides, leaps, and free-falls over a series of large stone slabs. The moderate volume of water begins as an 8-foot-wide branch and reaches a width of 40 feet by the time it drops to the base. The waters run under the road and continue down the mountain into one of the prongs of the Davidson River.

From the parking area, you will cross the Davidson River on an auto bridge and then come to a gravel road on your right, also marked as the Daniel Ridge Loop Trail. Go right here, avoiding the part of the loop trail that continues along the Davidson River. A gravel logging road ascends a hill and leads to the base of Toms Spring Falls. To the left of the falls is a trail marker for Daniel Ridge Trail, where it leaves the gravel road.

Thinking there was a different view of the falls, we hiked the moderate 0.4-mile slope. From the top, there was no view of the falls due to dense foliage, but the sound effects were great, and an excellent view of Looking Glass Rock opened before us. With water streaming down its sides and reflecting the sunlight, Looking Glass Rock stands like a lonely sentinel, rising 1,700 feet above the forest floor. The Daniel Ridge Trail continues past the top of the falls, where you can make a 4-mile loop back down to the parking area.

DIRECTIONS From the intersection of NC 280 and US 276 on the northeast side of Brevard, take US 276 north 5.2 miles and turn left onto FR 475 (Fish Hatchery Road). After 1.4 miles, you will pass the fish hatchery. Stay with FR 475, the lower gravel road that follows the river, for 1.9 miles. Continue past Cove Creek Campground 0.7 mile to the unmarked parking circle on the right.

GPS TRAILHEAD COORDINATES 35.284567, -82.827983

78 WATERFALLS OF GRAVEYARD FIELDS
[3.2-mile balloon, moderate]

A combination of high country and high, bold waterfalls is rare, but you can find it here along the Blue Ridge Parkway. Yellowstone Prong gathers and flows in the bosom of mile-high mountains, creating two visually exciting waterfalls. The hike linking Lower Falls and Upper Falls travels a medley of field and forest, rock and sky, delivering panoramas of the mountains from which the falls flow. *Note:* The area is very popular in summer. We suggest hiking early in the morning and

WATERFALLS OF GRAVEYARD FIELDS: LOWER FALLS

late in the evening then or during the shoulder seasons of spring and fall. In winter, this segment of the Blue Ridge Parkway often closes.

Join an asphalt trail leaving Graveyard Fields Overlook to soon bridge rock-filled Yellowstone Prong. Leave right from the bridge, toward Lower Falls. At 0.2 mile, pass a side trail that connects to the Mountains-to-Sea Trail before reaching a multitiered boardwalk that takes you to Lower Falls. This tiered waterfall stairsteps approximately 50 feet in four segments, each angled differently. At the bottom, a massive boulder jumble gets splattered, turning this spiller into mist. Adjacent dry boulders offer seating. Amazingly, you are at your lowest elevation yet are still more than 5,000 feet high!

To reach Upper Falls, backtrack, joining a new trail where you see a sign for Upper Falls. Most hikers visit Lower Falls and then return to their vehicles. However, Upper Falls *is* worth it. This is where the landscape catches your fancy. Wander through meadows, woods, and bogs. At 0.5 mile, the trail opens to views of the surrounding ridges: Graveyard Ridge, Black Balsam Knob, and Pisgah Ridge, where the Blue Ridge Parkway stands.

At 0.6 mile, reach a trail intersection. A user-created trail leads left to Yellowstone Prong, but you turn right and immediately come to another intersection, this one signed. Go left, toward Upper Falls, as the Graveyard Ridge Connector Trail keeps straight. The walking is easy up the Yellowstone Prong valley amid varying flora—pockets of yellow birch and maple, open blackberry brambles, grasses, and dark evergreen copses.

At 0.9 mile, reach another intersection. Stay right, still aiming for Upper Falls. The other way is your return route, to Graveyard Fields Overlook. Look back at the Graveyard Fields Overlook. Step over the quartz-pocked main tributary to Yellowstone Prong at 1.3 miles. After 1.5 miles, start climbing a bit. The path splits at 1.7 miles. Most hikers go left, down to an unnamed slide fall slipping over a rock face. Upper Falls is upstream, and you reach the many-faced falls at 1.8 miles. The horse-tail cataract pours 45 feet over tan bedrock and then fans out, only to make a brief direct drop and then fan out again on a wide rock slab. It briefly slows and then pushes onward. Upper Falls is visually striking, and the added effort weeds out the crowds.

Backtrack 0.9 mile from Upper Falls, and then join the loop leading back to Graveyard Fields Overlook. Bridge willowy Yellowstone Prong and ascend under sporadic spruces. The track aims for the Blue Ridge Parkway and delivers you to the road at 3.2 miles.

DIRECTIONS From the intersection of NC 280 and US 276 on the north end of Brevard, take US 276 north 15 miles to turn left onto the Blue Ridge Parkway. Follow the Blue Ridge Parkway 7 miles south to the Graveyard Fields Overlook, on your right at milepost 418.8.

GPS TRAILHEAD COORDINATES 35.320333, -82.847017

79 BUBBLING SPRINGS BRANCH CASCADES
[0.2-mile out-and-back, easy]

This waterfall, visible from the road, makes its splash where the headwaters of the West Fork Pigeon River and Bubbling Springs Branch meet.

The cataract, located at 4,800 feet elevation, exudes high-country splendor. It flows about 25 feet in two stages, flanked by spruces, yellow birches, and other vegetation that grows only on the highest mantles of the Southern Appalachians.

BUBBLING SPRINGS BRANCH CASCADES

Born on the slopes of 6,000-plus-foot Mount Hardy, astride the Blue Ridge Park-way, Bubbling Springs Branch dashes down the north slope of the Blue Ridge, culminating in a two-tiered frothy, stony drop into a rock-lined plunge pool.

To visit the falls, leave the parking pulloff and descend an eroded user-created trail, quickly reaching an overused campsite overlooking the West Fork Pigeon River, a mere creek—albeit scenic—backed by a rock bluff. Rock-hop the West Fork and arrive at the base of Bubbling Springs Cascades. An excellent array of sun-splashed stone slabs creates a wonderful viewing perch. A pool worthy of a chilly upland dip lies between you and the cascades. The überclear water flows over a sheet of naked rock, even at higher flows, forming a border between the flowing water and adjacent trees.

DIRECTIONS From Brevard, take US 64 West 8.4 miles to turn right onto NC 215 North. Continue on NC 215 North, crossing the Blue Ridge Parkway. Continue beyond the Parkway 1.8 miles to a pulloff on the right. The cas-cades are visible from the pulloff. *Note:* Start looking around 1.6 miles from the Parkway, and then head for the third pulloff on the right.

GPS TRAILHEAD COORDINATES 35.314370, -82.910336

80 COURTHOUSE FALLS
[0.6-mile out-and-back, easy]

Courthouse Falls is also called Coon Dog Falls. While on the hunt, a hound was swept away by the current and inadvertently took the plunge. Shockingly, this cataract has been successfully descended by daredevil kayakers who, like the lucky hound, lived to bark about it. Flowing through the Balsam Grove area of Pisgah National Forest, Courthouse Creek is a major tributary of the North Fork of the French Broad River. It charges through Summey Cove, picking up speed as the gradient increases.

The forceful water drops over a series of 5-foot ledges before reaching the precipice, where it is squeezed between rock outcrops and its power is released down a vertical rock face. The result is the magnificent 50-foot Courthouse Falls. The last 10 feet free-falls into a cauldron of bubbling, dark-green water. The granite walls at the base of the waterfall have been eroded by the circular flow of the current, creating an interesting whirlpool effect.

The Summey Cove Trail leads to Courthouse Creek Falls, following the creek along an abandoned railroad bed left over from World War I logging days. After 0.2 mile, take a left at the trail marker for the falls. This will lead you down a switchback to the base of the falls. Steep steps complete the access. The spur trail to the falls is about 0.1 mile.

Courthouse Creek originates around Devil's Courthouse Mountain. A Cherokee legend tells of a giant, slant-eyed devil named Judaculla who resided deep inside the mountain. Within his dark legal chambers, Judaculla passed final judgment on departing souls. This gateway to the spirit world was held in reverence by the Cherokee people, and the waters that emerged were considered sacred.

DIRECTIONS From the intersection of NC 215 and US 64 near Rosman, take NC 215 north for 10 miles. Turn right on Forest Road 140 (Courthouse Creek Road). Follow this sometimes-rough gravel road 3 miles. Immediately after the fourth bridge, park in the small pulloff on the right. The Summey Cove Trailhead is across the road to the right of Courthouse Creek.

GPS TRAILHEAD COORDINATES 35.273847, -82.892173

81 MILL SHOALS FALLS, FRENCH BROAD FALLS, AND CATHEDRAL FALLS
[0.6-mile out-and-back, easy]

Within the Balsam Grove area of Pisgah National Forest, two watersheds converge behind Living Waters, a Christian ministry, to form a double waterfall. The North Fork of the French Broad River flows from the northwest and tumbles over a river-wide rock shelf, creating a 60-foot curtain of water called French Broad Falls. Shoal Creek joins the French Broad from the northeast a short distance downstream as Mill Shoals Falls, the site of an old millhouse built by William McCall circa 1900.

These waterfalls are among the easiest and most accessible in the area. Plus, you drive right past them on the way to Courthouse Falls. Just leave the parking area and walk left, past the chalet building and along the shoulder of NC 215 about 40 yards. Turn right down an old roadbed to the river. This puts you behind the ministry buildings. (*Note:* The steps behind the chalet building have been blocked off for safety reasons.) You can stand on one of the many rocks at the base of the falls to view the 180-degree panorama of falling water. The roar from the waterfalls drowns out all sounds from the nearby road, giving you the impression of being in the middle of the wilderness.

Farther downstream, you will find the 20-foot Cathedral Falls, also called Bird Rock Falls. The name comes from the 100-foot granite cliff that served the nesting needs of hundreds of barn swallows.

DIRECTIONS From the intersection of US 64 and NC 215 in Rosman, drive north on NC 215 for 8 miles. Living Waters Ministries will be on the left; park in its lot. The waterfalls are on private land, so ask permission if possible before viewing, and then thank them when they say yes. (*Note:* The parking lot will be full if there is a retreat going on.)

GPS TRAILHEAD COORDINATES 35.224575, -82.861894

82 CONNESTEE FALLS AND BATSON CREEK FALLS
[0.1-mile out-and-back, easy]

Connestee Falls is often referred to as a double, or twin, falls. Actually, it is a three-tiered falls joined at its base by Batson Creek Falls, a separate cataract that enhances the appeal of a visit to Connestee Falls. The two cascades can be viewed together from a boardwalk situated astride the top of Connestee Falls, open to the public. The Carolina Mountain Conservancy purchased the land around the falls, and it is now a Transylvania County Park. Today, we view the two falls from the top looking down. Remain on the boardwalk.

Emanating from Lake Atagahi, Carson Creek pours a hefty 16,000 gallons a minute over three rock ledges that form Connestee Falls. Modest Carson Creek broadens into a 25-foot-wide drape of roaring water as it drops over the first and most precipitous ledge. The waters plunge a total of 110 feet before merging with the output from Batson Creek.

Originating from Lake Ticoa, Batson Creek emerges from the south to glide over a granite dome and also drops 110 feet, creating Batson Creek Falls. Batson Creek Falls has less volume than Connestee Falls. However, when the creeks converge and are squeezed between two rock walls, the result is a wild sluice of water known as the Silver Slip. The consolidated waters journey north and eventually join the French Broad River.

Carson Creek was named after Revolutionary War veteran John Carson, who began his military career fighting the Cherokee people until a greater enemy came along, the South Carolina Tories. In 1795, after the war for independence was won, Carson moved to Transylvania County and acquired a large parcel of land adjacent to the creek that bears his name.

The land changed hands many times during the ensuing years. William Probart Poor, Brevard's prominent judge, once paid $5 for 100 acres on Carson Creek, which included a then-unknown shoals. This shoals later became known as Connestee Falls. Probart Street in Brevard was once named Poor Street in honor of Judge Poor. Due to local objection, the name was changed to the judge's middle name. It seems that no one liked the idea of living on Poor Street.

Connestee Falls got its name from a beautiful Cherokee princess who jumped to her death after her white husband was lured back to live among his people. It has been rumored that her brokenhearted spirit still roams the scene of her demise. On moonlit nights at the place where the two waterfalls become one, you would not be the first to catch a glimpse of the woeful Princess Connestee.

DIRECTIONS From downtown Brevard, take US 276 south 6 miles to Connestee Falls, on your right. A large parking lot serves both the Top of the Falls Realty Office and the boardwalk to the falls.

GPS TRAILHEAD COORDINATES 35.164861, -82.730409

83 HOOKER FALLS, TRIPLE FALLS, AND HIGH FALLS
- **Hooker Falls** [0.5-mile out-and-back, easy]
- **Triple and High Falls** [1.8-mile out-and-back, moderate]

Many people come to DuPont—the most visited of North Carolina's state forests—to see its waterfalls, especially since Triple Falls and Hooker Falls were featured in the 2012 film version of *The Hunger Games*. The 10,300-acre state forest south of Brevard was established in 1996. Outdoors enthusiasts and the grassroots organization Friends of DuPont Forest played a big role in saving the area's waterfalls in 2000, when the forest was expanded. The state forest includes the upland

High Falls

plateau of the Little River Valley, which is mostly mixed hardwood forest with sections of white pine. Along with the waterfalls, some of DuPont's highlights include the exposed granite domes, such as the one on 3,600-foot Stone Mountain, and the picturesque Lake Julia.

The state forest encompasses more than 80 miles of trails for horseback riders, hikers, and mountain bikers. In addition to the four waterfalls on the Little River (the three profiled here, plus Bridal Veil Falls on page 177), there are also two waterfalls on Grassy Creek: Grassy Creek Falls and Wintergreen Falls, detailed on pages 174 and 176, respectively.

Hooker Falls requires the shortest hike and provides wheelchair access. Part of the original land acquisition for the state forest, it is a popular swimming hole and the former site of a gristmill. Start the hike by passing the gate and following the wide path marked HOOKER FALLS ROAD. When you intersect the paved wheelchair access, bear left, staying on the dirt-and-gravel path. At the top of the falls, continue straight for a good view from an observation area. The 13-foot waterfall drops over a very wide ledge and eventually flows into Cascade Lake. Hooker Falls is considered the fourth waterfall on the Little River.

Triple Falls and High Falls—numbers three and two on the Little River, respectively—are upstream from Hooker Falls. From the same parking lot, cross the Little River on a 120-foot-long pedestrian bridge, and then pass under the highway bridge. Follow the trail upstream as it parallels the river and remains level for the first part of the hike. Following a bend to the right, you will ascend steeply. At about 0.3 mile, you can view Triple Falls to the left from the viewing area or to the right from the picnic shelter. A side trail farther up on the left uses steps to reach the pool between the second and third drop. The three tiers of Triple Falls add up to 120 feet.

Continue upstream and uphill another 0.5 mile to reach High Falls. The trail will intersect High Falls Trail; head left. At the next trail intersection, go right and up a moderately steep climb to view High Falls. The steps to the right lead up to High Falls Shelter for an excellent view. To reach the base of the falls, take the River Bend Trail. High Falls, the tallest in DuPont State Forest, slides down a granite dome for about 150 feet.

DIRECTIONS From downtown Brevard, take US 276 south 11.0 miles to Cascade Lake Road in Cedar Mountain. Look for the Cedar Mountain Volunteer Fire Department. Turn left onto Cascade Lake Road and follow it 2.5 miles to Staton Road/Forest Road 1591. Turn right on Staton Road and follow it 2.5 miles to the Hooker Falls trailhead, located on your left just after the bridge over the Little River. (*Note:* You will pass the High Falls trailhead on your right after 1.4 miles on Staton Road. It could be used as an alternative access.)

GPS TRAILHEAD COORDINATES 35.202777, -82.619090

84 GRASSY CREEK FALLS
[3.0-mile out-and-back, moderate]

This cataract is overshadowed by more prominent cascades within DuPont State Forest, namely those on the Little River such as High Falls and Triple Falls. As its name indicates, this 40-foot angled cascade is on Grassy Creek, a tributary of the Little River. On days when the falls on the Little River are hopping with hikers and swimmers, head to Grassy Creek Falls to soak in a sun-splashed waterslide flowing into a deep pool, where you'll enjoy more elbow room, whether you are practicing your waterfall photography, simply seeking a contemplation rock, or looking for an uncrowded swimming hole.

The hike to the falls is a fine one too. The trail system at DuPont State Forest is fully signed and developed, and it can be busy. Hikers, mountain bikers, and equestrians ply the pathways here. Most of the route to Grassy Creek Falls is on doubletrack Lake Imaging Road, which is gated and open only to forest personnel. Leave the large parking area, and then pass around a pole gate, joining Lake Imaging Road. The level track enters rich woods and quickly circles around a tributary of Hooker Creek. Cruise east and at 0.3 mile reach Lake Imaging. The word *lake* is a bit ambitious for this diminutive but scenic pond of 2 acres, located at the confluence of Hooker Creek and Jim Branch. A covered shelter adds picnicking possibilities.

Lake Imaging Road circles left around the lake and then crosses Jim Branch. At this point you leave the water and angle south up a wooded hillside. The path works over some open rock slabs before reaching the crest of the ridge dividing Jim Branch from Grassy Creek at 1.2 miles. Here, the Hilltop Loop leaves right. It

GRASSY CREEK FALLS

also provides access to Grassy Creek Falls but adds 0.5 mile to the hike. The shorter, easier route stays straight on Lake Imaging Road. It gradually descends to reach another intersection at 1.4 miles. Turn right here, joining the Grassy Branch Falls Trail. The narrower path soon intersects the other end of the Hilltop Loop and then narrows into a singletrack footpath, with steps aiding the descent. Grassy Creek is singing below. Oddly, you will come to an old stone grill in a small flat above Grassy Branch Falls. A short spur leads to the top of Grassy Creek Falls. Here, you can peer down the sliding slice of stream. In all but the highest flows, most of the water pours down the right side of the slide. Grassy Creek then flows into big boulders, feeding a sizable and relatively deep pool.

DIRECTIONS From downtown Brevard, take US 276 south 11.0 miles to Cascade Lake Road in Cedar Mountain. Look for the Cedar Mountain Volunteer Fire Department. Turn left onto Cascade Lake Road and follow it 2.5 miles to Staton Road/Forest Road 1591. Turn right on Staton Road and follow it 2.9 miles to the Lake Imaging Trailhead, on your right.

GPS TRAILHEAD COORDINATES 35.209283, -82.615133

85 WINTERGREEN FALLS
[3.2-mile out-and-back, moderate]

Wintergreen Falls is the forgotten waterfall of DuPont State Forest. We've never seen another soul there on our visits. Yes, this cataract is the least spectacular of the cascades at DuPont, but it does afford the most solitude and a nice hike as well.

The first order of business is figuring out which way to go from the large Guion Farm access. Start your waterfall walk by heading south from the trailhead kiosk, traversing through open field. At 0.1 mile, enter white-pine woods in the southwest corner of the field, and walk a doubletrack path to meet Tarkiln Branch Road. This "road," like many other trails at DuPont, is open only to park personnel. Turn right on Tarkiln Branch Road, immediately passing a spur horse-watering trail. The doubletrack then crosses Tarkiln Branch and turns south, cruising through its piney valley. Watch for short side trails leading to grassy wildlife clearings, as well as old roads shortcutting the official trail.

Descend the drainage to reach a trail intersection at 1.0 mile. Here, Tarkiln Branch Road leads right for lower Tarkiln Branch. Stay left, joining the

WINTERGREEN FALLS

Wintergreen Falls Trail. The path gently descends in oaks and pines scattered with big boulders. At 1.3 miles, come to another intersection. Stay left with the Wintergreen Falls Trail as the Sandy Trail dips to run alongside Grassy Creek, which is now clearly audible.

After passing a horse hitching post, the Wintergreen Falls Trail leads to the densely wooded banks of Grassy Creek. Boulders and mountain laurel tangle the forest floor. The trail narrows and snakes up the bank. Work through rhododendron and mountain laurel, and then emerge at the lower end of Wintergreen Falls, located at a bend on Grassy Creek. You will likely pop out well below the falls, getting an almost side view of the 15-foot spiller as it tumbles over a wide rock wall, slowing in a boulder-pocked pool before rushing fast en route to the Little River. A smaller, shorter drop adds a little spice to the cascade.

Some deft footwork will take you to open boulders revealing a head-on view of Wintergreen Falls. A mix of sun and shade presents good perches no matter the season. At lower water levels, the pool below the falls will be good for swimming, but when roaring, it runs too swiftly.

DIRECTIONS From downtown Brevard, take US 276 south 11.0 miles to Cascade Lake Road in Cedar Mountain. Look for the Cedar Mountain Volunteer Fire Department. Turn left onto Cascade Lake Road and follow it 2.5 miles to Staton Road/Forest Road 1591. Turn right on Staton Road and follow it 4.9 miles to Sky Valley Road (Staton Road turns into DuPont Road toward the end). Turn right on Sky Valley Road and follow it 1.5 miles to the Guion Farm trailhead on your right.

GPS TRAILHEAD COORDINATES 35.211433, -82.587950

86 BRIDAL VEIL FALLS
[4.0-mile out-and-back, moderate]

Bridal Veil Falls, the first waterfall on the Little River in DuPont State Forest, requires a longer hike than Hooker, Triple, and High Falls (page 171), but it is worth the trip. From the Fawn Lake Access Area, pass the yellow gate next to the information board, reach the sign marking Reasonover Creek Trail, and go right, walking under the power lines. At the marked intersection, take a left on the wide Conservation Road. You will pass a green metal gate and the Shortcut Trail on the left. Then walk parallel to an old airport runway and hangar, and finally pass Camp Summit Road, a house, and Lake Julia Road, all on the right. Take a left on Bridal Veil Falls Road, passing a barn on the left. The gravel road ends, but you'll continue straight ahead on the 0.1-mile trail through pine trees toward the falls.

This 120-foot waterfall, with its 10-foot unusual overhanging top—the bridal veil—and long sliding lower section, is on the 2,200-acre tract on the south side of the state forest, part of the acquisition in 2000. You can walk under the 4-foot overhang at the base of the falls, sunbathe on large rock slabs, and enjoy the pool at the base.

DIRECTIONS From downtown Brevard, take US 276 south 11.0 miles to Cascade Lake Road in Cedar Mountain. Look for the Cedar Mountain Volunteer Fire Department. Turn left onto Cascade Lake Road and follow it 0.1 mile to turn right on Reasonover Road. Follow this road 2.8 miles to Fawn Lake Access Area. Turn left and go uphill, passing four large stone pillars, and then take an immediate left into the gravel parking area.

GPS TRAILHEAD COORDINATES 35.160750, -82.604000

BRIDAL VEIL FALLS

87 RAVEN CLIFF FALLS
[7.9-mile loop, strenuous]

This challenging loop hike takes you to a well-visited overlook of famed Raven Cliff Falls and then loops around to see the falls as few do. The trip is arduous but separates you from the rest of the crowd in the Mountain Bridge Wilderness. However, you can turn this into a 4.0-mile out-and-back trek, gaining a distant but clear view of Raven Cliff Falls.

Leave the trailhead and registration area, descending on a gravel road. The Foothills Trail runs in conjunction with the Raven Cliff Falls Trail here. Pass a power line clearing and outbuilding, and then veer right, now on a foot trail that follows an old roadbed. The wide dirt track meanders westerly on the cusp of a deep drop-off into Matthews Creek, and the path features great winter views to the south. You can hear the stream and falls roaring below.

The nearly level track travels over some rock slabs in a pine–oak–laurel forest. At 0.9 mile pass side trails leading left to slabs with few views. Descend into a rhododendron thicket, and then rise back into dry wood to pick up a straight roadbed at 1.3 miles. Veer left, keeping southwest to reach a junction at 1.5 miles. Here, the Foothills and Raven Cliff Falls Trails part ways. The Foothills Trail will be your return route.

Stay with the Raven Cliff Falls Trail, descending via switchbacks, still on the edge of the drop-off. Watch for a rock bench at one switchback. You will meet the Dismal Trail in a gap at 1.9 miles, but keep following the Raven Cliff Falls Trail for 0.1 mile to reach a rock overlook and a wooden viewing platform. Through a frame of trees, you can see 400-foot Raven Cliff Falls dropping over a sheer rock face. It is a long-range vista; binoculars would come in handy here. Backtrack to the purple-blazed Dismal Trail and begin your big descent. This singletrack footpath shows much less use. Soon pass an outcrop that offers a superior view of Raven Cliff Falls. The path switchbacks down a steep slope amid small trees crowding the trail.

Keep aiming for Matthews Creek loudly crashing below. Trees and shrubs thicken before meeting the Naturaland Trust Trail at 3.3 miles. This is the low point of the hike, below 1,800 feet. Turn right here, heading upstream in evergreens. Continue up the gorgeous remote valley to reach a crossing of Matthews

Creek. Here, you can see big rocks, frothing water, and pools in this mountain watercourse, which cuts an incredible gorge. At normal flows, Matthews Creek can be rock-hopped, but just in case, double steel cables are tightly strung across the creek for high-water, high-wire-act crossings. The cable crossing is actually fun and challenging.

Climb away from Matthews Creek, leaving the streamside environment. The bouldery track makes an irregular ascent on a singletrack footpath. You are way above the creek, ultimately reaching a cliff line. The second cliff line you reach is simply incredible. The rock wall heads straight up for the sky, leaving mere mortals puny by comparison.

Beyond the bluff, the climbing remains relentless and uses ladders and steps to gain ground. Emerge onto an outcrop at 4.2 miles. The view of upper Matthews Creek and the mountains upon which you will shortly be walking is inspiring. Below you, and mostly out of sight, Raven Cliff Falls is simply roaring. Relax here and take it all in. Be careful—the drop is a doozy.

Switchback uphill more, on a laurel- and galax-lined path, soon coming across a rock shelter, left of the trail. It could come in handy during a rainstorm. Work your way forward on a narrow, rooty track, and then meet Matthews Creek and a costly and incredible suspension bridge. It stands above the uppermost fall of Raven Cliffs Falls, which you can see. Downstream, the main drop of Raven Cliff Falls disappears over a rock rim, with a sheer mountain as backdrop. Upstream are more cascades of Matthews Creek, which continues displaying superlative beauty.

Beyond the span, the Naturaland Trust Trail continues up the upland valley of Matthews Creek before curving away from the creek to enter hickory-oak–pine woods, tracing an old roadbed. Meet the Foothills Trail at 4.7 miles. Turn right here, heading uphill on an eroded rocky and sandy track. The Foothills Trail levels off and then offers easy highland cruising. It takes a little while for your ears to adjust to the quiet after leaving the continual rushing-water roar of the Matthews Creek valley.

You are now back above 3,000 feet, and your legs feel it. Take your time and enjoy the woods here, tramping in the high country, now atop the mountains you were looking at earlier from the outcrop beside Raven Cliff Falls.

Leave high pinewoods for dark rhododendrons to cross a small stream by culvert at 5.5 miles. Rise from the stream shed to make an abrupt right turn at 6.0 miles, soon climbing past a gate to meet the Raven Cliff Falls Trail at 6.4 miles. Begin backtracking here, returning to the trailhead at 7.9 miles.

DIRECTIONS From downtown Brevard, take US 276 south 14.1 miles to Raven Cliff Falls in South Carolina, reaching the parking area on the left 2 miles after crossing the state line. Use the parking fee kiosk at the trailhead. Hiker registration is also required. The well-marked trailhead is on the right side of the road opposite the parking area.

GPS TRAILHEAD COORDINATES 35.115604, -82.638050

RAVEN CLIFF FALLS   *photo: Sherry Jackson*

Cashiers

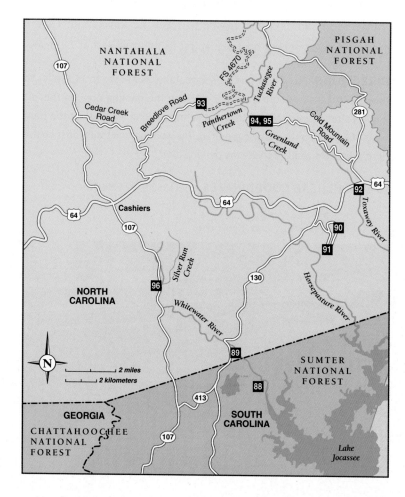

88 LOWER WHITEWATER FALLS
[4.4-mile out-and-back, moderate]

Most waterfall enthusiasts head for easy-to-reach Whitewater Falls. However, its downstream cousin, Lower Whitewater Falls, makes its own case for visitation. In my opinion, Lower Whitewater Falls is one of the most remarkable falls in the United States, which is saying a lot. Some may call it blasphemy, but Lower Whitewater Falls is even more beautiful than Whitewater Falls. Solitude lovers take note: Lower Whitewater Falls sees one-tenth of the foot traffic that Whitewater Falls does.

Leave the large Bad Creek Access parking area, taking the Bad Creek Access Trail, a graveled, brushy path bordered by scrubby trees, grass, and regrowth over disturbed land. Whitewater River loudly roars from your right before it is stilled as part of Lake Jocassee. Keep east through more brush until the trail comes under the canopy of a mature forest at 0.2 mile. The Bad Creek Access Trail skirts the west side of a small knob and gently descends into a flat, where you can hear the Whitewater River again. Drift across the wooded riverside flat to reach a trail junction and the first of two bridges over the Whitewater River at 0.6 mile. The Coon Den Branch Trail leaves left. Keep straight, bridging the Whitewater River, to meet the Foothills Trail.

Stay straight on the Foothills Trail, heading toward Lower Whitewater Falls Overlook. The other way heads upstream on the Whitewater River. Shortly span a small branch on a bridge, and then leave the riverside flat it has been crossing. Make a trail junction 1.2 miles from the Bad Creek Access Trailhead. Here, you leave the Foothills Trail and join the Lower Whitewater Falls Access Trail. From here to the falls overlook, the path skips off and on old dirt and gravel roads. However, the blazed trail is well marked and well used.

Keep forward, traversing a small knob, and then turn left, following a red-dirt track beyond a metal gate. At the gate, turn right, and then make a quick left, joining a bona fide gravel road, Musterground Road, open to the public in fall hunting season. The wide, pea gravel track makes for easy hiking, but you leave the road 0.3 mile from the Foothills Trail junction, a total of 1.4 miles from the trailhead. This is a right turn away from the gravel road.

LOWER WHITEWATER FALLS

Pines, sourwoods, and canes border the trail as it gently climbs the west slope of Whitewater Mountain. You cannot help but wonder where the trail is going as you ascend and no longer hear water. The trail reaches a high point and begins a gradually steepening downgrade totaling 300 feet. The sounds of rushing water fill your ears. At 2.2 miles, reach the Lower Whitewater Falls Overlook.

Now you are face-to-face with Lower Whitewater Falls, which drops across a chasm lying between you and it. The Whitewater River makes a few warm-up tumbles, just for kicks, and then makes a final practice drop before diving off a sheer ledge in a roaring sheet of white bordered in gray granite and framed in dense forest, with mountain ridges and sky beyond. The general claim is that the waterfall is 400 feet high, with its upstream brother Whitewater Falls being 411 feet high. That last sheer drop is just so impressive.

DIRECTIONS From the intersection of US 64 and NC 107 in Cashiers, take NC 107 south, entering South Carolina and intersecting SC 413. Turn left on SC 413, and follow it 2.5 miles to meet SC 130. Stay left, joining SC 130. Follow SC 130 for 0.9 mile to the gated entrance to the Bad Creek Project, on your right. Drive up to the gate and it will open (6 a.m.–6 p.m.). Pass through the gate and continue downhill 2.1 miles. Turn left at the sign for the Foothills Trail, driving 0.3 mile to a large parking area. The Bad Creek Access Trail starts in the far left corner of the parking area.

GPS TRAILHEAD COORDINATES 35.011475, -82.999813

89 WHITEWATER FALLS
[0.6-mile out-and-back, easy]

This is the king of waterfalls. Immense and spectacular, the aptly named Whitewater River plunges 411 feet over the sheer granite cliffs of the gorge. The ground seems to shake as the sound of crashing water echoes in the valley. The falls tumble in a frame of oak, poplar, maple, and hickory trees, the constant spray creating a home for various ferns and mosses.

Whitewater Falls is arguably the most photographed waterfall in the Southern Appalachians. Deserving of its accolades, the cataract tumbles in an irregular series of chutes, pitches, and slides, ever widening until it finally stops in a furtive vapor of spray and mist. Beyond this falls, the Whitewater River continues its chaotic descent, entering South Carolina to fill Lake Jocassee.

The Nantahala National Forest has built a large parking and picnic area for the congregation of waterfall enthusiasts. Solitude seekers can visit during off-times: mornings, weekdays, and cold weather. First, grab a view from the parking lot into the Whitewater River Valley and beyond into South Carolina's foothills.

An asphalt path leads 0.25 mile to the all-access overlook of Whitewater Falls. Peer forth to the cataract below. Initially, Whitewater Falls flows in a relatively slender chute; then it pours down a less steep angle, fanning over bedrock. The best part of the falls comes last, where it spreads and steepens, echoing up to this perch, stilling among spray-slickened boulders.

For a closer vantage, take 152 steps, including the landings between actual steps, to the lower overlook. This perch presents a nearer vista, as close as the hostile terrain permits. Preserved hemlocks border the wooden viewpoint. To your right, the set of stairs leaving the lower overlook connects to the Foothills Trail.

It is 111 more steps to reach the Foothills Trail (FT). The FT begins to switchback via more steps into the depths of the Whitewater Gorge. Downstream you see giant boulders clogging the river as the water loudly forces its way downstream. After 0.5 mile, an iron suspension bridge allows you to cross the Whitewater River and adds a great watery view. The Foothills Trail goes on, and the 90-mile track is the pride of the Palmetto State's upstate pathways.

DIRECTIONS From the intersection of US 64 and NC 107 in Cashiers, take NC 107 south, entering South Carolina and intersecting SC 413. Turn left on SC 413 and follow it 2.5 miles to meet SC 130. Stay left, joining SC 130. Shortly return to North Carolina and reach the Whitewater Falls parking area on your right. *Note:* After you reenter North Carolina, SC 130 turns into NC 281.

GPS TRAILHEAD COORDINATES 35.029439, -83.016329

WHITEWATER FALLS   *photo: Nicole Blouin*

90 UPPER BEARWALLOW FALLS
[0.5-mile out-and-back, moderate]

Once called Snakerock Falls, Upper Bearwallow Falls is part of Gorges State Park. Visitors can access a vista of the whitewater pour-over via the Bearwallow Falls Trail. Gorges State Park is characterized by the rugged terrain of the Blue Ridge Escarpment, with dramatic elevation changes up to 2,000 feet in 4 miles, plunging rivers, remote gorges, and sheer rock walls. There are more than a dozen falls in the park, some on the Toxaway River and Bearwallow Creek and others on their tributaries and other smaller streams. You can access the spectacular Gorges section of the Foothills Trail from the other side of the park, where several deep rivers course down into Lake Jocassee. Upper Bearwallow Falls, just inside the park's northwestern boundary, drops about 80 feet in several stairsteps. It is one of the most beautiful waterfalls in Transylvania County. The trailhead has water, restrooms, and a shaded picnic shelter. The trail switchbacks down to a long vista of the falls.

Leave the Bearwallow Falls picnic area, immediately crossing the park loop road. The 4-foot-wide path descends into the Bearwallow Falls gorge on a southeast-facing slope amid pines, mountain laurel, galax, and chestnut oaks. At 0.1 mile, make the first of several switchbacks taking you on a steep but doable grade. Resting benches are situated along the way.

After 0.25 mile, come to an overlook of Upper Bearwallow Falls. You have descended almost 200 feet. The overlook delivers a clear but long vista of the falls. Take a few minutes enjoying the view not only of the falls but also of the nearby mountains and lowlands of South Carolina beyond. Binoculars will enhance your vista of the falls.

DIRECTIONS From Cashiers, take US 64 east about 9 miles to NC 281. Turn right and take NC 281 for 1 mile to the Gorges State Park entrance, on your left. Enter the park and reach the visitor center after 1 mile. The road splits just after the visitor center. Head left and follow the road 0.9 mile to the Bearwallow parking area and picnic shelter on your right.

GPS TRAILHEAD COORDINATES 35.101400, -82.945350

91 WATERFALLS OF THE HORSEPASTURE RIVER

 ◊ **Stairway Falls** [2.4-mile out-and-back, moderate]
 ◊ **Rainbow Falls** [3.0-mile out-and-back, moderate]
 ◊ **Turtleback Falls** [3.2-mile out-and-back, moderate]
 ◊ **Drift Falls** [3.6-mile out-and-back, moderate]

Before October 27, 1986, the Horsepasture River was in danger because a power company was planning to build a hydroelectric dam that would terminate the water flow to the falls. But Friends of the Horsepasture River, with the help of legislators and state organizations, won their fight to block the project. A section of river 4.5 miles long was designated Wild and Scenic to be protected by the federal government.

The river plunges almost 2,000 feet over 6 miles in a dramatic series of wide drops and boulder-filled rapids. Additionally, the Horsepasture River is a waterfall collector's heaven; four outstanding cascades can be seen here.

Gorges State Park is your starting point for this four-star waterfall adventure. Stairway Falls is the shortest option from the Gorges State Park parking area. A user-created path spurs off the Rainbow Falls Trail and leads 0.4 mile to the base of Stairway Falls. The peaceful nature of the falls is captivating, quite a change from the powerful Rainbow Falls. Several stairsteps, averaging 10 feet each, add up to a total drop of just over 50 feet.

But the Horsepasture's showstopping cataract is Rainbow Falls, a near-vertical drop of 200 feet. The entire river crashes onto the boulders below, producing a deafening roar. If the sun is just right, you may see colorful arches created in the spray; hence the name Rainbow Falls. Your best bet to see a rainbow is to visit the falls during a clear winter morning. It is truly a magnificent cataract.

Upstream from Rainbow Falls, you will first find Turtleback Falls. In the summer, a large swimming hole and a natural waterslide draw in hikers and swimmers. However, do not swim in the moving water between the Turtleback Falls swimming hole and Rainbow Falls—especially at high water. Fools continue to be swept over Rainbow Falls while playing around the water below Turtleback Falls, a dangerous proposition at best, lethal at worst.

Beyond Turtleback Falls, you can walk upstream to view 80-foot Drift Falls, which is posted NO TRESPASSING. Do not go to or past Drift Falls, an angled slide cascade. Public land ends at the pool just below the falls. You can come within photography range, but don't go beyond the property boundary. Respect the rights of private landowners.

Your ticket to the waterfalls—Rainbow Falls Trail—leaves the large parking area, cruising a piney ridge. At high flows, the Horsepasture River is already audible. At 0.3 mile, reach a trail intersection. The Raymond Fisher Trail leads left to backpack campsites. You stay right with the Rainbow Falls Trail as it curves into a tributary of the Horsepasture River. Keep a downgrade. Maples and rhododendron add to the vegetation. Rock-hop a small tributary at 0.6 mile. At 0.8 mile, leave Gorges State Park to enter Pisgah National Forest. The trail becomes a bit more primitive.

At 1.0 mile, officially enter the Wild and Scenic River corridor. Here, a trail leads left to Stairway Falls. To access Stairway Falls, trace this narrow user path left, down the nose of a ridge lined in laurels and pines. Soon reach a flat and campsite along the Horsepasture River. Curve left here, tracing the river downstream. Rock-hop the same tributary you crossed earlier. From here, the user-created trail becomes primitive but well worn. Snake your way among rocks, roots, and vegetation on a steep slope. At 1.2 miles, you emerge at the river, just at a sharp bend, and the lowermost "step" of Stairway Falls. Gray boulders provide perches for looking up at the stairs and the pools that divide them.

The hike to Rainbow Falls is on a marked, maintained, and improved trail, including wood-and-earth steps that ease the footwork. Starting at the split from the route to Stairway Falls, the Rainbow Falls Trail drops to another tributary and a campsite in a flat, at 1.1 miles from the trailhead. Continue up the right bank of the Horsepasture River, which spills in shoals and minifalls, slows in pools, and generally lives up to its Wild and Scenic status.

The path is forced away from the water on a high bluff, then you come back along the river. At 1.4 miles, come near a huge, deep pool bordered by large, gray relaxing rocks. A low curtain-type fall, more wide than tall, feeds this deep hole. It is sometimes known as Hidden Falls because thick vegetation shrouds the falls from the trail. Keep up the rugged river gorge. At 1.5 miles, you come to Rainbow Falls and the open upper viewing area, bordered by a wooden fence. A mist splashes onto the viewing area, as well as onto the waterfall viewers themselves. A wet, open slope stretches to the base of the falls.

The maintained trail continues and leads down to a spray-covered and slippery path to a lower observation platform. This is one of those waterfalls that sticks in my mind and bolsters my enthusiasm for cataracts.

To access Turtleback Falls, stay right beyond the spur to the lower overlook of Rainbow Falls. Continue working your way up the right side of the Horsepasture River. Come near the top of Rainbow Falls, but exercise caution. Then reach Turtleback Falls, 20 feet or so high, at 1.6 miles. On summer weekends, throngs of swimmers and rock waterslide enthusiasts gather, watching each other slip down the wet slope into the pool from granite slabs bordering the waterway. It is advisable to swim here only at lower river flows.

Drift Falls is farther upriver. Continue up the trail, reaching a private-property boundary and sign. Drop left here to the Horsepasture to view the 70-foot falls, also known as Driftwood Falls and Bust-Yer-Butt Falls, from the old days when it was used as a daredevil rock waterslide. Suppress the temptation to explore upstream—again, it's private property.

DIRECTIONS From Cashiers, take US 64 east about 9 miles to NC 281. Turn right and take NC 281 for 1 mile to the Gorges State Park entrance on your left. Enter the park and reach the visitor center after 1 mile. The road splits just after the visitor center. Stay right and follow the road 0.6 mile to a large parking area and Rainbow Falls trailhead on your right.

GPS TRAILHEAD COORDINATES 35.088783, -82.951850

92 TOXAWAY FALLS
[mileage and difficulty not applicable]

"Wow, look at that!" is a common reaction from unsuspecting motorists who round the corner on US 64 between Sapphire and Brevard and come upon Toxaway Falls. Though the volume of water is low compared to some of the other falls in Transylvania County, the view of the falls and the river gorge below is incredible. After a full day of waterfall trekking, the tired hiker may also appreciate that Toxaway Falls is visible from the car.

From the dam that impounds Lake Toxaway, the Toxaway River runs under the concrete bridge, and the falls begin their near-vertical plunge at 3,000 feet above sea level. Water slides 125 feet over a massive dome-shaped granite shelf, and halfway down, a curved rock causes the current to spout upward and form a huge rooster tail. The Toxaway River continues its turbulent path over numerous cascades and cataracts on its 1,500-foot descent through the picturesque Toxaway River Gorge, finally relaxing once it reaches the backwaters of Lake Jocassee.

Many people believe that the falls, river, mountain, and lake were named after the famous Cherokee leader Toxawah. The name Toxaway was also linked to an American Indian settlement in the area; however, the spelling on the old maps and deeds was Toxawah. Prevailing legend puts the grave of Toxawah at the top of Indian Grave Ridge, which is approximately 0.75 mile from the top of Toxaway Falls.

The destruction from the flood of 1916 is still visible. The sweeping torrent cleared the heavy riverside vegetation and exposed the massive granite domes. The landscape may be altered, but the view from the top of the falls is still breathtaking. The waterfall now marks the boundary line for Gorges State Park. The demarcation is obvious: the west side of the falls and the shoreline are built up with condominiums, while the east side remains natural.

DIRECTIONS Toxaway Falls is just downstream from Lake Toxaway Dam. US 64 cuts between the dam and the falls. You can't miss it. Use the restaurant parking lot just west of the falls for a good view, or use an access point just east of the falls and walk out on the boulders for a closer view. Extreme caution is advised.

GPS TRAILHEAD COORDINATES 35.123900, -82.931100

93 WATERFALLS OF WESTERN PANTHERTOWN VALLEY
♦ Wilderness Falls, Frolictown Falls, and Granny Burrell Falls
[3.4-mile out-and-back, moderate]

The 6,300-acre Panthertown Valley Backcountry is rife with aquatic beauty in its falls and on the land through which its streams course. A century back, the valley was logged, but the forests have recovered nicely. Set in the headwaters of the Tuckasegee River, the land was bought with a resort in mind, but nothing materialized. At one point, it seemed that the Blue Ridge Parkway would go through here, but the road never did make it this far south. Duke Power saw the land as a corridor for its power-line system and purchased the tract, then ran its giant transmission lines on a rough northwest–southwest axis. Still, the splendor of the terrain could not be denied, and the Nature Conservancy procured the area not contained within the power-line right-of-way and transferred the tract to the Nantahala National Forest. Today, we can all enjoy this water-rich slice of the Blue Ridge on a trail network of 30 miles.

This hike begins on the wide Panthertown Valley Trail. It is an easy walk on an old roadbed, but that changes after 0.2 mile. Here, you turn right on the Wilderness Falls Trail. (If you keep straight on the Panthertown Valley Trail, it soon opens to a grand vista of the greater Panthertown Valley.) Your route turns to singletrack trail as it descends a fern-filled valley. Dip near a stream, then drift onto a dry ridge and meet the first of the seemingly innumerable open rock slabs for which Panthertown Valley is known. The trail works its way down along Wilderness Falls via a rerouted path that was once much steeper. Wilderness Falls is a long, narrow granite slide cataract on Double Knob Gap Creek. The entire 80-foot drop is partially obscured by dense mountain laurel. The waterfall trek resumes a more level pace as it traces Frolictown Creek.

At 1.1 miles you will meet the Deep Gap Trail, which leaves right to cross Frolictown Creek and left toward Panthertown Creek. Take a spur trail straight and down to Frolictown Falls, a graceful, camera-attracting waterfall. It spills about 15 feet over a smooth rock face, shaded by lush greenery in a mossy, rocky cathedral. Sandbars frame the plunge pool. To make your way to the next waterfall, return to the four-way intersection and head right on the Deep Gap Trail, coming to the Great Wall Trail at 1.2 miles. Stay right on the Great Wall Trail and enter a wide forested flat. Cross Frolictown Creek at 1.5 miles and come to yet another intersection. Here, head left on the Granny Burrell Falls Trail. You are now walking along Panthertown Creek, as Frolictown Creek has added its waters upstream. Mountain laurel and rhododendron intertwine in lush thickets. At 1.7 miles, come to Granny Burrell Falls, which presents a distinct contrast to the cascades you have seen thus far. The pour-over glides gently about 16 feet over naked granite, collects, and stops. Then Panthertown

FROLICTOWN FALLS

Creek escapes, flowing atop more bedrock, to stop again in a dusky pool, surrounded by sand enough for a beach. This is a popular swimming and sunning area in the summertime.

> **DIRECTIONS** From the intersection of US 64 and NC 107 in Cashiers, take US 64 east 1.9 miles to Cedar Creek Road. Turn left on Cedar Creek Road. In 2.2 miles turn right on Breedlove Road. (There is a sign for Panthertown Valley Backcountry Area here.) In 3.3 miles, Breedlove Road appears to dead-end, but veer left to join a downhill gravel track. Reach the trailhead in another 0.2 mile.
>
> **GPS TRAILHEAD COORDINATES** 35.167917, -83.040117

94 SCHOOLHOUSE FALLS
[2.6-mile out-and-back, easy–moderate]

Simply stated, Schoolhouse Falls is a prototype waterfall, my mental mold of the exemplar cataract. It has a crisp, clean drop and a large plunge pool amid an alluring mountain setting. And it is this compilation that makes the falls such a draw, here within the Nantahala National Forest's popular Panthertown Valley Backcountry Area, northeast of Cashiers.

The hike to the falls is a breeze, too, with a drop of just over 250 feet. (Of course, you regain the elevation on your return.) Your adventure starts at the Cold Mountain Trailhead, the primary eastern gateway to the Panthertown Valley, a land of not only waterfalls but also granite domes sporting extensive vistas, plus lush, dense forests primed with much precipitation that also keeps the waterfalls flowing. The Panthertown Valley Backcountry Area trail system was once a mess, but thanks to Friends of Panthertown, a volunteer organization, the trail system has been straightened out and is well marked and maintained, aided by personnel of the Nantahala National Forest.

SCHOOLHOUSE FALLS

Two trails leave from the trailhead, which is located at more than 4,000 feet elevation. Leave right with the Panthertown Valley Trail. Cruise through upland hardwoods, skirting the edge of a development known as Canaan Land. At 0.2 mile, the trail meets a primitive road and leaves left. (The roadbed leading right enters Canaan Land.) Emerge onto a power-line clearing, and then reenter woods. The contrast between the open clearing and dark forest will be stunning in the height of summer. The wide track then makes a pair of switchbacks, making the downgrade easier. The forest thickens with more moisture-loving species, led by rhododendron. At 1.0 mile, the Devils Elbow Trail leaves right, but you keep straight and cross a sturdy bridge over Greenland Creek. Just beyond here, the trail splits. Stay left, joining the narrower Little Green Trail, so named because it eventually climbs to the open granite peak of Little Green Mountain, shadowing Schoolhouse Falls.

The path enters mountain wetlands, vegetated feeder streams, and overflows of Greenland Creek. A boardwalk over part of the wetlands keeps the plants untrampled and waterfall visitors' feet dry. At 1.3 miles, the Little Green Trail splits right to climb Little Green Mountain, but you keep straight as the trail opens to Schoolhouse Falls. Boulders standing atop gravel form a viewing stand. Beyond stretches a tea-colored pool, much larger than Greenland Creek could seemingly deliver. Scads of rhododendron, complemented by deciduous trees, overhang the swimming hole. In the distance, Schoolhouse Falls pours in a neat, white curtain, falling 20 feet over a stone lip. If you don't mind getting a little wet, you can even walk behind the falls. In the cool of a shady morn, Schoolhouse Falls makes for an ideal photograph setting—and you will beat the crowds.

DIRECTIONS From Cashiers take US 64 east 9 miles to NC 281. Turn left onto NC 281 North and follow it 0.8 mile to turn left on Cold Mountain Road, just past the Lake Toxaway Fire and Rescue Station, on your right. Follow Cold Mountain Road 5.6 miles to turn left on a marked gravel road just before reaching the Canaan Land residential development. Follow this marked gravel road 0.1 mile, and turn right on a signed gravel road. Follow it 0.1 mile to dead-end at the trailhead.

GPS TRAILHEAD COORDINATES 35.157733, -82.998896

95 GREENLAND CREEK FALLS
[2.2-mile out-and-back, easy–moderate]

True, Greenland Creek Falls plays second fiddle to its downstream cousin, Schoolhouse Falls, here in the Panthertown Valley Backcountry Area. But this pour-over is a worthwhile destination in itself. Plus, you arguably take a more scenic trail to Greenland Creek Falls, and a nearby waterfall—Macs Falls—can be accessed along the way. To reach Greenland Creek Falls, leave the trailhead on the hiker-only Greenland Creek Trail. It passes around a pole gate and then bisects a wide power-line clearing. The now-shaded path works toward Greenland Creek in rich forests of oak. Come to a trail split at 0.3 mile. Here, a user-created side path sneaks under mountain laurel to 12-foot Macs Falls. This smaller cascade delivers tea-colored water over a wide rock slab into a plunge pool. The area is difficult to access. Pothole Falls, about 10 feet high and set in a narrow alcove, is a little farther downstream, and this unofficial trail also leads to it.

Return to the main trail, and shortly reach mountain laurel–choked Greenland Creek. This evergreen grows in dense thickets most of the way upstream to Greenland Creek Falls. White pines tower above it all. Macs Gap Trail, a multiuse path coming from the same trailhead, comes in at 0.7 mile. Stay right, continuing upstream along Greenland Creek. Macs Gap and Greenland Creek Trails run in conjunction here. At 0.8 mile, in a small clearing, reach another intersection. Macs Gap Trail leaves right to ford Greenland Creek, but you keep straight on the Greenland Creek Trail. The hiking gets interesting here, as the sometimes muddy path snakes through extreme laurel thickets, through which clear streamlets wind. Without warning, you burst forth from the thickets to find Greenland Creek Falls. A boulder jumble provides natural spots for repose as you observe the cataract spilling 30 feet atop a flared rock face into dark, still water deep enough for submersion.

DIRECTIONS From Cashiers take US 64 east 9 miles to NC 281. Turn left onto NC 281 North and follow it 0.8 mile to turn left on Cold Mountain Road, just past the Lake Toxaway Fire and Rescue Station, on your right. Follow Cold Mountain Road 5.6 miles to turn left on a marked gravel road just before reaching the Canaan Land residential development. Follow this

GREENLAND CREEK FALLS

marked gravel road 0.1 mile, and turn right on a signed gravel road. Follow it 0.1 mile to dead-end at the trailhead.

GPS TRAILHEAD COORDINATES 35.157733, -82.998896

96 SILVER RUN FALLS

[0.4-mile out-and-back, easy]

Silver Run Falls is thankfully just within the boundaries of the Nantahala National Forest. And so is the parking and the trail to the falls, making a trip here both legitimate and fun. The trail to Silver Run Falls is almost completely level. Halfway to the falls, you cross a small creek on a footbridge. Just downstream, the small creek joins Silver Run Creek. These two creeks are part of the headwaters of the Whitewater River, where you'll find fabled Whitewater Falls.

After following the sound of rushing water under hardwoods for several hundred yards, the trail brings you out to several rocks ideal for viewing this 25-foot falls. The blue-green water pours into a large, circular pool, creating an inviting and popular swimming hole that is open to the sun overhead. Silver Run Falls is surrounded by a damp forest of rhododendron, mountain laurel, and tulip trees.

DIRECTIONS From the intersection of US 64 and NC 107 in Cashiers, drive south on NC 107 for 4.0 miles, where you will see a sign and a bridge for the falls on the left. The trailhead is at the utility pole, and the waterfall is in the Nantahala National Forest. Be apprised that the gravel pulloff has limited room. Please consider other cars when parking.

GPS TRAILHEAD COORDINATES 35.066866, -83.066930

Highlands

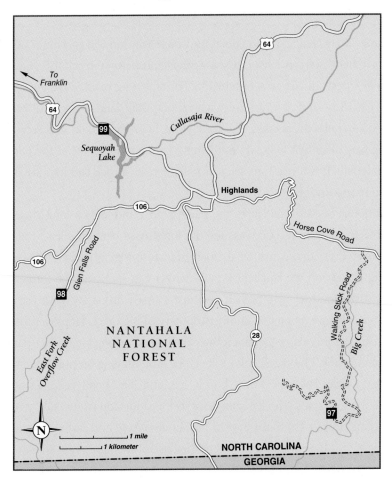

97 BIG SHOALS, AKA SECRET FALLS
[1.2-mile out-and-back, easy]

Previously, hikers heading to this falls found their way on old logging roads and skirted—ahem, perhaps even crossed—private property to reach this Nantahala National Forest aquatic gem. But the U.S. Forest Service realized the visual value of this cataract—and of forest users staying on public lands—and thus built the Big Shoals Trail, which takes you to 35-foot-high Big Shoals, aka Secret Falls (by the way, *Secret Falls* is slowly but surely claiming the mantle as the name for this waterfall). It is a real tumbler, too, spilling over a rock cliff into an alluring sand-bordered pool.

The Big Shoals Trail leaves the parking area and joins a long-closed and now-overgrown forest road. Pass the old forest road gate on a level track. The Big Shoals Trail curves around a small branch, bridging it via a culvert. The walking is easy on the singletrack path, which was laid over the former road. Pines crowd the trail. The branch you just crossed drops away. Cruise under white pines before dipping to another tributary of Big Creek. Hop over the small stream and shortly come to yet another small creek. A long log bridge spans this mountain brook. The Big Shoals Trail climbs a bit, staying on public land. Hit a gap at 0.5 mile. The trail drops sharply left, and Big Shoals becomes audible. Ahead, the trail splits. The left spur goes to the stony top of the falls, while the official trail drops right to the base of Big Shoals. Wood and earth steps aid your footing as you trace the official trail to the base of the falls.

At 0.6 mile, emerge from under mountain laurels to rocks, sand, and a fine observation point. Here, Big Shoals froths its way over a cliff. The main thrust of water drops on the right, but the left side has enough flow to keep an array of plant life clinging to cracks and crevices. A greenish pool deepens below the falls and provides dipping opportunities. Below the pool of Big Shoals, an angled stairstep cascade curves around a corner. Big Creek soon enters Georgia and flows onward to form West Fork Chattooga River, which then flows into the main stem of the Chattooga at the Georgia–South Carolina boundary.

DIRECTIONS From downtown Highlands, at the intersection of Main Street and US 64, near the NC 28 intersection with US 64, take Main Street east. Main Street becomes Horse Cove Road. Follow it over a ridge and into Horse Cove

3.7 miles to Walkingstick Road/NC 1608. Turn right on Walkingstick Road. Follow the unpaved road past cabins, fording a small stream without benefit of a bridge at 2.5 miles, then bridge Big Creek just after passing Rockhouse Road on your left. At 2.9 miles, turn right onto Forest Road 4567. Climb a bit and then come to the Big Shoals Trail parking area on your left at 0.2 mile.

GPS TRAILHEAD COORDINATES 35.007483, -83.166083

98 GLEN FALLS
[1.8-mile out-and-back, moderate–strenuous]

Enjoy four separate viewing points of Glen Falls, but begin with a mountain vista. Three of the four waterfall overlooks are developed decks, and each of the four aquatic vistas presents a different frothy expression. The reported height of Glen Falls varies because it is hard to figure out where one fall starts or ends or even if it is one endless cataract. Be careful here; too many people have perished playing around Glen Falls. Stay on the trail and be prudent. The open rock slabs are slick and angled.

GLEN FALLS

Leave the trailhead on the Glen Falls Trail on a wide, gravel, all-access path. White pine, mountain laurel, and rhododendron form an evergreen backdrop. At 0.1 mile, the level trail comes to a highlands overlook. Enter the East Fork Overflow Creek valley and reach your first observation deck at 0.2 mile. East Fork careens down an angled slope and then spills away beyond sight. Ahead the trail splits. Take the path leading acutely right, back toward East Fork. At 0.4 mile, find the second observation deck at the base of the upper falls. Above, East Fork charges over a wide stone bluff and then eases into a more subtle, angled drop before flowing out of sight again. Look for the observation deck you saw earlier.

At 0.7 mile, reach the next observation deck, which is perched along the creek's edge. This is my favorite fall. It fans out in tiers about 65 feet over widening bedrock. Here, the developed part of the Glen Falls Trail ends, but another worthwhile waterfall can be seen downstream. The path becomes riddled with roots as it heads away from the creek. At 0.8 mile, the Glen Falls Trail leads left to an alternate trailhead on Forest Road 79C in Blue Valley; turn right, dropping to East Fork Overflow Creek to reach the final cataract. This curtain fall spills 15 feet into a punchbowl, where you can safely enter the water. Here ends the nonstop drop of East Flow Overflow Creek, and the pool is a receptacle for natural debris pushed down by big rains.

> **DIRECTIONS** From the intersection of US 64 and NC 106 in Highlands, take NC 106 south 1.8 miles to turn left on Glen Falls Road. The access road to Glen Falls veers right, just after the left turn from NC 106. Follow Glen Falls Road 1.0 mile to dead-end at the trailhead. Parking is limited, so be considerate about how and where you park your vehicle.
>
> **GPS TRAILHEAD COORDINATES** 35.033300, -83.235850

99 WATERFALLS OF THE CULLASAJA GORGE
- **Kalakaleskies Falls** [mileage and difficulty not applicable]
- **Bridal Veil Falls** [mileage and difficulty not applicable]
- **Dry Falls** [0.3-mile out-and-back, easy]
- **Lower Cullasaja Falls** [mileage and difficulty not applicable]

The Cullasaja Gorge is one of God's masterpieces. It would be difficult to find a more rugged river gorge anywhere in the Blue Ridge. The Cullasaja River runs parallel to US 64 between Highlands and Franklin. Considered one of the most beautiful routes in western North Carolina, this stretch of highway, a National Forest Scenic Byway, was carved into the side of a cliff.

To build the road, workers were repeatedly lowered from clifftops in rope slings to drill holes and place dynamite to blast away solid granite. Construction began in 1928, and in 1929, an estimated 2,000 people attended a ceremony to unveil a monument to the founder of Highlands, Samuel Kelsey. The first gravel was unloaded in 1931, and the road was partially paved by 1932. It is a wonder that the work was ever completed. The federal government denied funds due to the extreme expense, and delays came from the road department because the employees were not enthusiastic about starting the hardest project of their careers.

LOWER CULLASAJA FALLS   *photo: Shutterstock/Colin D. Young*

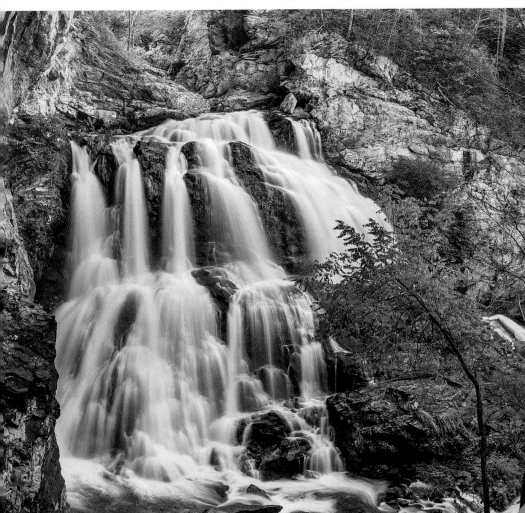

The road construction has allowed us to witness the Cullasaja River's unspoiled beauty and tremendous power. Stating that the river descends close to 2,000 feet in 7.5 miles should tell the story, but there are also ripples and rapids, twists and turns, and many drops. These drops add up to several major falls and a dozen minor ones, each with its own personality. Daredevil kayakers take on the river's rapids and falls.

Just below the dam on Lake Sequoyah at the upper end of the gorge, a series of small waterfalls is collectively known as the Kalakaleskies. Scramble down the bank to the river's edge and explore. This is the beginning of the many waterfalls on the Cullasaja River.

The dam was built in 1927 and measures 28 by 175 feet. It creates the 66-acre lake named after the famed American Indian chief Sequoyah. This Tennessee hunter and fur-trading native, who never attended school, developed a system of writing that enabled the Cherokee to publish books and newspapers in their own language.

The next waterfall comes with a legend. American Indian maidens believed that if they walked behind the falls in the spring, they would marry before the first snowfall. From that came the name Bridal Veil. You once could drive under the waterfall. Traffic was routed along the paved semicircle behind the falls before the construction of US 64.

DRY FALLS   *photo: Shutterstock/Jon Bilous*

Bridal Veil is a delicate falls; the water volume is small. The upper section clings to an 80-foot rock face, and the lower section free-falls about 40 feet. Bridal Veil Falls is incredible in the winter, when frozen spray adorns the plants and icicles cling to the overhang. Because this waterfall is just 100 feet off the highway, it is the most well-known and photographed waterfall around Highlands.

Dry Falls boasts a very dry back side, which is where it gets its name—and its popularity. It is possible to walk under the falls without getting wet because of a hollow area that has been cut away by centuries of erosion. You can look out into the Cullasaja Gorge through the sheets of water. (*Note:* Be prepared to get soaked if the river is running high.)

A set of steps and a paved walkway will take you to the viewing area. The river plunges 75 feet from a protruding shelf onto rocks just a few feet from the path. The constant spray irrigates rare plants such as rock club moss and Appalachian filmy fern. There is a sensational roar.

Do not turn back to Highlands until you have seen the last major water-fall in the gorge; it is a blockbuster. Lower Cullasaja Falls is higher and more captivating than any of the others. It crashes through the steep canyon over a series of wide ledges and then falls freely for 150 feet. The river splits into several dramatic cascades, each worthy of its own name. Dropping a total of 250 feet in 0.25 mile, Lower Cullasaja Falls is considered one of the most picturesque falls in North Carolina.

The best vantage point is from a paved shoulder off US 64. An unmaintained path will get you closer, but it is difficult, requiring the use of your hands and feet. Fortunately, the view from the shoulder is stunning. This may not be a perfect place for a picnic, but your photograph is sure to be striking.

DIRECTIONS From Highlands, head northwest on US 64 toward Franklin. Within 2 miles, you will be driving alongside Sequoyah Lake, and the dam will be visible on the left. Kalakaleskies covers a 0.25-mile stretch below the dam, and there are several places to stop. Bridal Veil Falls is next on your right; there is a paved circular pulloff. Travel another 0.9 mile to the parking area for Dry Falls on your left. And finally, pull off on the shoulder after 5.5 miles to view Lower Cullasaja Falls. No sign marks the area, but you can't miss the falls. It is best to pass the falls, turn around, and come back to park.

GPS TRAILHEAD COORDINATES 35.067950, -83.225167

Franklin

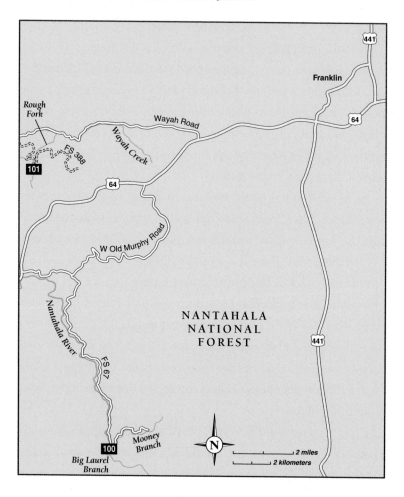

100 BIG LAUREL FALLS

[1.0-mile out-and-back, easy]

Big Laurel Falls is a highlight of the greater Standing Indian Area and Southern Nantahala Wilderness Area. A high-quality campground makes for a great base to explore a well-marked and maintained trail system, the backbone of which

BIG LAUREL FALLS

is the Appalachian Trail. Big Laurel Falls is a fanning cataract set in a rock glen. We recommend viewing the falls in all seasons. It is one of those special places worth coming back to time and again.

The hike starts at 3,700 feet elevation. The easy walk departs the parking spot on Forest Road 67 and drops to Mooney Creek, a mountain rill noisily coursing among mossy boulders. Span the stream on a bridge to reach a trail junction; turn right toward Big Laurel Falls. Walk downstream on an old railroad grade, and then turn up Big Laurel Branch on a narrow footpath through tunnels of laurel, from which rise gnarled birch and cherry trees. The hollow, rich with spring wildflowers, closes tighter. Come to Big Laurel Falls at 0.5 mile. Here, the multitiered cataract makes a drop and spills over an expanding rockslide into a reflecting pool. Rhododendron borders the cascade and pool. This path dead-ends here and will likely whet your appetite to take in more of the Standing Indian Area and the Southern Nantahala Wilderness Area.

DIRECTIONS From the intersection of US 23/US 441 and US 64 in Franklin, take US 64 west 12 miles to West Old Murphy Road. There will be signs for Standing Indian Campground. Turn left on West Old Murphy Road and follow it 1.9 miles to turn right onto Forest Road 67. Follow FR 67 for 6.8 miles to the Timber Ridge and Laurel Falls trailhead, on a left curve, passing Standing Indian Campground and the Backcountry Information Center on the way.

GPS TRAILHEAD COORDINATES 35.021917, -83.503433

101 RUFUS MORGAN FALLS
[1.0-mile loop, moderate]

The Rufus Morgan Trail, a short loop, is cut out of a mountainside. You will encounter some steps, as well as narrow tread and stream crossings, and will pass through a mature hardwood stand to reach the waterfall. Rough Fork Creek slides down a 70-foot drop into a small pool surrounded by ferns.

From the trailhead, pick up the blazed trail, and ascend up and to the right to encounter some switchbacks. You will reach a small stream crossing at 0.2 mile and intersect an old logging road. Continue straight ahead on the trail (not the wide dirt road) and descend. At 0.4 mile, cross Rough Fork Creek at the base of a small warm-up falls. From there, walk upstream toward the small cascading waterfall. In winter, Rufus Morgan Falls is visible, uphill and upstream. Switchbacks ascend to the falls.

The waterfall and the trail are named for Albert Rufus Morgan, a naturalist and a minister who loved the mountains. Often called the one-man hiking club, he worked on trails in the area, including the Appalachian Trail, for a quarter century. He died in 1983 at the age of 97. We should heed the example set by such a man.

Instead of returning the way you came, turn right and mostly descend on switchbacks to finish the loop, emerging on Forest Road 388, within sight of the trailhead.

DIRECTIONS From the intersection of US 23/US 441 and US 64 in Franklin, take US 64 west for 3.8 miles; turn right on Old Murphy Road. Drive 0.2 mile, then turn left on Wayah Road/NC 1310. Follow NC 1310 for 6.6 miles, passing Arrowhead Glade Picnic Area at 3.3 miles. Turn left onto FR 388. After 2 miles, look for a small pulloff on the right and a sign indicating the Rufus Morgan Trail. *Note:* FR 388 is closed in the winter.

GPS TRAILHEAD COORDINATES 35.146300, -83.547933

Great Smoky Mountains
National Park and Cherokee

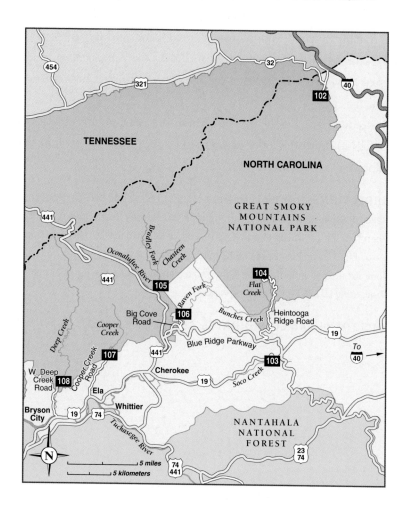

102 MOUSE CREEK FALLS
[4.0-mile round-trip, easy–moderate]

This Smoky Mountain waterfall trek leads past swimming holes, big trees, and the everywhere-you-look splendor of ultraclear Big Creek en route to 40-foot Mouse Creek Falls. Big Creek valley has returned to its original state of forest primeval. Before our time, this area was once home to native Cherokee and Scotch-Irish settlers; then it was a timber source and camp for loggers, then a place where young men of the Civilian Conservation Corps built trails, including the one upon which we walk to Mouse Creek Falls, a thrilling cataract that makes its dive just before Mouse Creek adds its flow to Big Creek.

MOUSE CREEK FALLS IN WINTER

Mouse Creek Falls in summer

Proceed up the Big Creek Trail, tracing what has been an American Indian path, a settlers' wagon road, a logging railroad, an auto road, and now a horse and footpath again. Saddle alongside Big Creek at 0.9 mile. View the trailside blasted rock where the gorge pinches the path against the steep mountainside, broken by impressive boulder fields rising up the mountainside. Note the color of Big Creek. Depending on depth and time of year, it displays an array of blues and greens that can look almost tropical. Reach Midnight Hole at 1.5 miles. Here, a cascade splits two boulders and flows into a swimming hole big enough for an army of sweaty hikers.

Continue uptrail. Flanks of rhododendron border the pathway. Take a second to look over now-nearby Big Creek. Massive midstream boulders stand worn smooth by Big Creek's endless rush. At 2.0 miles, reach the short spur trail leading left to Mouse Creek Falls and a horse-hitching post. This fall is located across Big Creek and is Mouse Creek's last hurrah before joining the waters of Big Creek. Here, Mouse Creek, draining the highlands of Mount Sterling Ridge, emerges as a narrow flow in a rhododendron thicket and then makes a two-tiered descent. The 40-foot cataract widens on its first drop, forms a pool, and then dives one more time before meeting its mother stream. Ample boulders provide resting and observation posts.

DIRECTIONS From I-40 northbound just west of the North Carolina state line, take Exit 451; turn left under the interstate and then right to reach a bridge across the Pigeon River on your left (if southbound on I-40, the exit ramp takes you directly to the bridge, where you turn right). After crossing the bridge, turn left to follow the Pigeon upstream. In 2.3 miles come to an intersection and keep straight to enter Great Smoky Mountains National Park. Pass the Big Creek Ranger Station and drive to the end of the gravel road and the hiker parking area. The Big Creek Trail starts on the left just before the hiker parking area.

GPS TRAILHEAD COORDINATES 35.751778, -83.110000

103 FLAT CREEK FALLS

[3.8-mile out-and-back, moderate]

This is another of those "Why aren't more people hiking this trail?" waterfall hikes. Maybe it's due to the fact that the Flat Creek Trail begins on a less-traveled road. But for waterfall enthusiasts there should be no maybes about walking this path. It starts at over 5,300 feet and passes a wonderful view of the Smokies crest before entering a high-country forest of spruces and yellow birches. The path then descends to the highland valley of Flat Creek and makes its way to the highest-elevation falls accessible by trail in the Great Smoky Mountains National Park. Enjoy a respite from the broiling lowlands during summer. June will offer the most water in Flat Creek and a more robust falls. Autumn features colors that contrast with the spruce trees and clear skies for awesome views.

Join the Flat Creek Trail as it swings around Heintooga Picnic Area. At 0.1 mile, near a water fountain, come to a cleared view at Heintooga Ridge Overlook. The crest of the Smokies stands north, and binoculars reveal Clingmans Dome tower. Soon reach a trail junction; the wide track continuing straight heads to the picnic area restrooms, but you drop right on a narrow hiker-only path. Overhead are regal straight spruces, their reddish trunks supporting boughs of evergreen, complemented by yellow birches, with their trademark horizontal peeling bark. Cherry, beech, and maple trees add to the woodland mix. The deciduous tree trunks can be twisted and distorted by powerful winter winds. Blackberry bushes grow wherever the sun penetrates the tree cover. Ferns and grasses are scattered about the forest floor.

At 0.8 mile reach Flat Creek, a small highland stream easily crossed on a footbridge. Keep a level course through pleasant woodland, crossing a tributary on a footlog at 0.9 mile. Rock-hop Flat Creek twice in succession at 1.1 miles. The surroundings change minute to minute. First, you may be in grassy deciduous woods, then under tall spruces, and next in a rhododendron thicket. It is all striking. Reach the side trail for Flat Creek Falls at 1.8 miles. Turn right here on a faint spur, as the main track continues toward Heintooga Ridge Road. Descend to Flat Creek. Keep kids under close supervision in this area, as Flat Creek puts gravity to work on its way to meet Bunches Creek in the valley below. Views of the Bunches Creek watershed open near Flat Creek. The cut of Heintooga Ridge Road is visible. Side trails on both sides of the creek lead to the steep, narrow 200-foot falls. It is challenging to get a complete view of the entire cascade, as the cataract is narrow and drops down a heavily vegetated rock chute.

DIRECTIONS From Cherokee, head north on US 441 for 2.8 miles, and turn right onto the Blue Ridge Parkway before the entrance to Great Smoky Mountains National Park. Follow it 10.9 miles to turn left on Heintooga Ridge Road. Travel 8.7 miles to the Heintooga Picnic Area. The Flat Creek Falls Trail starts at the end of the auto turnaround near the picnic area. Heintooga Ridge Road is generally open mid-May–October.

GPS TRAILHEAD COORDINATES 35.573133, -83.180233

104 SOCO FALLS
[0.1-mile out-and-back, easy]

Soco Falls is a dichotomy of nature's splendor and man's trash. Unfortunately, the area around the pulloff and trail was once a convenient dumping ground, though it is a little better loved these days. "Take only memories; leave only footprints" was never more applicable. Is Soco Falls worth a visit? Yes! You may also wish to bring an empty trash bag. A trip here reminds us that the preservation of beauty is the responsibility of those who treasure it.

Soco Creek and a larger unnamed creek converge at right angles just south of Soco Gap to form an unusual 40-foot double waterfall called Soco Falls. As you face the falls, you will notice Soco Creek entering from the left while the main cascade emerges from the shade, high above you. Leaping into full view, the water reflects the rays of the midday sun, creating a sparkling spectacle. The two creeks meet midway in their nosedive to the pool at the base of the falls. Soco Creek then flows into the Oconaluftee River.

From the trailhead, you can hear the falls. A family-friendly trail leads you to an observation deck and view. Going to the base of the falls is not recommended because it involves climbing down a near-vertical embankment. Some people do, creating messy paths and leaving ropes behind on their descent. Don't do it!

Soco is derived from the Cherokee word *sogwo*, meaning "one." Legend links the name to Hernando de Soto, the Spanish explorer. Supposedly, the

American Indians shouted "Soco!" as they threw one of de Soto's soldiers over the falls to his death.

Soco Gap, the junction of US 19 and the Blue Ridge Parkway, marks the boundary of the Qualla Reservation. This was the initial point of the 1876 US survey that created the reservation. Soco Gap is also referred to as Ambush Place, where the Cherokee wiped out a raiding party of Iroquois.

DIRECTIONS From Cherokee, travel about 10.5 miles north on US 19, toward Maggie Valley. Look for the Soco Falls sign and gravel parking area 1.4 miles before you reach the Blue Ridge Parkway.

GPS TRAILHEAD COORDINATES 35.492967, -83.170183

105 CHASTEEN CREEK CASCADES
[4.0-mile out-and-back, moderate]

This hike leads from Smokemont Campground, open year-round. The trek travels along Bradley Fork, former home to pioneers eking out a living on streamside flats. The creek displays superlative mountain stream scenery. You will then turn up a tributary, Chasteen Creek, to find a waterfall waiting. The entire walk is bathed in national park–level scenery. The mostly wide and gentle graded trail is good for families, though horses can muck up flat spots along Chasteen Creek.

Leave Smokemont Campground on the Bradley Fork Trail. To your left Bradley Fork crashes, dashes, and splashes over water-worn gray rocks. On higher ground, mossy boulders and ferns lie beneath a forest heavy with locust and tulip trees taking over former inhabited clearings. Try to imagine the home-sites that once occupied these flats along Bradley Fork. Cross a wooden bridge over Chasteen Creek. Beyond this crossing, at 1.2 miles, is the Chasteen Creek Trail junction. Turn right here, heading up a smaller valley. Pass the Lower Chasteen backcountry campsite #50 at 1.3 miles. It offers wooded and partly open camps with Chasteen Creek to sing you to sleep.

Keep up the wooded valley, bridging Chasteen Creek. Wildflowers abound in spring. Meet a spur trail and horse hitching post at 2.0 miles. Here, Chasteen Creek makes a 20-foot tumble over a rock face. Depending on the flow, the waterfall sometimes splits into separate ribbons as it pours over the rock. Mossy boulders provide green contrast where water isn't flowing.

DIRECTIONS From the Great Smoky Mountains National Park Oconaluftee Visitor Center near Cherokee, drive 3.2 miles north on US 441. Turn right and bridge Oconaluftee River toward Smokemont Campground. Veer left, and then turn right again to pass the Smokemont Campground check-in station. Bradley Fork Trail starts at the gated jeep road in the rear of the campground. In winter, parts of the campground may be gated, so you may have to park closer to the check-in station.

GPS TRAILHEAD COORDINATES 35.563063, -83.310771

106 MINGO FALLS AND UPPER MINGO FALLS

◆ **Mingo Falls** [0.8-mile out-and-back, moderate]
◆ **Upper Mingo Falls** [0.6-mile out-and-back, strenuous]

Mingo Falls and Upper Mingo Falls, located on the Cherokee Indian Reservation, are a most impressive sight. Collectively, they are one of the highest waterfalls in the area, dropping 120 feet, this is not the only feature that sets it apart from other falls. The water seems to fall in slow motion. This surreal effect is created by the stratified sandstone ledges, hundreds of tiny stairsteps in the rock face that slow the water.

Pigeon Creek Trail, which leads you to these cascades, is within the Cherokee Indian Reservation. The first several hundred yards are fairly steep, including 161 steps, and then the trail levels off at the base of Mingo Falls. A separate spur trail, much less used, takes you to Upper Mingo Falls, spilling 30 feet in two main segments and much wider than Mingo Falls. *Note:* With a smallish watershed these falls flow low in late summer through autumn.

DIRECTIONS From Cherokee, go north on US 441 for 2.3 miles to turn right on Big Cove Road. Follow it 4.5 miles. Mingo Falls Campground is on the right. The campground is tribal property, and non–campground users are welcome to park in the designated area. Pigeon Creek Trail begins behind the campground water system.

GPS TRAILHEAD COORDINATES 35.534133, -83.276167

107 LITTLE CREEK FALLS
[3.6-mile out-and-back, moderate]

In many areas of life, there is a direct correlation between effort and reward. Little Creek Falls is no exception. You may be slightly winded or have tired legs from climbing the steep switchbacks by the time you get to the falls, but following this section of trail over streams and through dense rhododendron thickets is half the fun.

Little Creek cascades down hundreds of small sandstone shelves for a total height of 95 feet. The rock staircase magnifies the volume of the relatively small mountain stream as water dances from shelf to shelf. At the base of the falls, there is a small pool where you can almost reach out and touch the falls. If you go 20–30 feet beyond the bridge, you'll get a more level perspective.

From the national park entrance point, take the Cooper Creek Trail. The creek itself marks the park boundary; you are on the west side of it. The trail roughly follows an old road subject to washout. The trail and creek intermingle a bit, which makes deft rock-hopping necessary if you wish to keep your feet dry. Cross Little Creek and reach the Deeplow Gap Trail at 0.6 mile. Settlers once lived in the area, near the confluence of Little Creek and Cooper Creek. Turn left on the Deeplow Gap Trail, leaving Cooper Creek behind for Little Creek. The trail becomes steeper as you climb toward Thomas Ridge for 1 mile. After two more creek crossings and several switchbacks, the sound of rushing water tells you the falls are just around the bend. From the far side of the pool at the base, the trail continues 0.2 mile to the top of the falls.

DIRECTIONS From the intersection of US 19 and US 441 in Cherokee, drive west on US 19 for 5.1 miles to the community of Ela. Turn right at the Cooper Creek General Store, and follow Cooper Creek Road 3.3 miles. (The pavement ends after 1.3 miles; bear right and stay along the creek.) You are looking for a trout-rearing farm. Please park at the gravel area across from the chain-link gate. Then you must sign in at the trout farm and be off the property by 4 p.m. Begin by walking through the gate at the boundary for the Great Smoky Mountains National Park.

GPS TRAILHEAD COORDINATES 35.492617, -83.370683

108 WATERFALLS OF DEEP CREEK

♦ Juney Whank Falls, Indian Creek Falls, and Tom Branch Falls

[2.4-mile loop, easy–moderate]

Visit three attractive waterfalls centered on Deep Creek and its tributaries within the bounds of Great Smoky Mountains National Park. Winter and spring are best for seeing these waterfalls at their boldest, and they are also the best time to experience solitude. Water lovers should come here during summer, but note that many others will be enjoying the aquatic features with you, including tubers on Deep Creek.

This hike begins at the developed Deep Creek area, with its campground and picnic facilities, located on the park's edge near Bryson City. The Juney Whank Falls Trail leads uphill in rich woods, climbing along Juney Whank Branch. It isn't long before you reach the slender, two-tiered, 18-foot cataract that spills in a slender ribbon over a rock face and then goes under the trail before making a second dive toward Deep Creek. Beyond here, the hike wanders back to Deep Creek before it travels up another tributary—Indian Creek. Indian Creek Falls—25 feet in height, but wider than it is tall—spills into a large pool. Next, you will return to Deep Creek, enjoying its beauty before coming to yet another tributary, Tom Branch. Tom Branch makes an 80-foot dramatic, rocky plunge as it meets Deep Creek. A little more waterside walking returns you to the parking area. Avoid this hike in the summertime if you disdain crowds. In summer, lower Deep Creek can be crazy with tubers floating from the confluence of Indian Creek and Deep Creek through the Deep Creek Campground and beyond the park border.

The Juney Whank Falls Trail starts out as a wide gravel path leading from the parking area. Juney Whank Branch calmly flows to your right after pouring off Beaugard Ridge. Shortly veer away from the watercourse, climbing to meet the Deep Creek Horse Trail at 0.1 mile. Watch for horses here, as a nearby concessionaire uses this route for a short distance. Stay right with the equestrian path in the second-growth woods of maple, pine, buckeye, beech, and tulip trees.

Reach the spur trail to Juney Whank Falls after 0.25 mile. Turn right and descend a hill to reach a bridge and the falls. The low-flow cascade spills close enough to the bridge with a built-in observation deck and seat so that you can

Tom Branch Falls

nearly touch the water. This waterfall will be at its most dramatic during winter when it's frozen, and in spring, when it flows strongest.

Leave Juney Whank Falls, and pass a shortcut leading right, down to Deep Creek. Rejoin the Deep Creek Horse Trail. Travel in pine–oak woods, turning up a quiet hollow. Dogwoods are plentiful here.

Reach a high point and a gap at 0.8 mile. The Deep Creek Trail drifts toward Hammer Branch, following a trickling tributary. Curve to step over fast-flowing Hammer Branch as a spur trail leaves to a pioneer cemetery. This hike then bridges Hammer Branch to meet the Deep Creek Trail at 1.4 miles. Watch for bicycles in the next section, primarily during summer. Deep Creek flows broad and boisterous as you cross the stream on a wide bridge. Span Indian Creek to meet the Indian Creek Trail at 1.5 miles.

Your second waterfall stands a football field distant, up the Indian Creek Trail. An access path leads to the base of this broad, tumbling froth of whitewater. Indian Creek Falls plunges over a rock face into a pool open to the sky overhead. While here, grab a top-down view from the Indian Creek Trail too.

Your return trip leads down Deep Creek. The trail travels well above the creek, where you can look directly into the water. The path drops creekside and then bridges Deep Creek.

At 2.2 miles, reach your final cataract. Benches make a perfect observation point to see Tom Branch stairstep over a series of rock ledges, finally meeting Deep Creek. From here, the hike returns to the parking area after 0.2 mile.

DIRECTIONS From Cherokee, take US 19 South 10 miles to Bryson City. Turn right at the Swain County Courthouse onto Everett Street. In 0.3 mile, as you leave Bryson City, veer right onto Water Street and continue 1.7 miles to a T intersection, where you turn left to reach the national park in 1.2 miles. Inside Great Smoky Mountains National Park, veer left toward a sign that reads TRAILHEAD, WATERFALLS. Juney Whank Falls Trail starts at the upper end of the trail parking area before you reach the auto turnaround above the parking area.

GPS TRAILHEAD COORDINATES 35.464228, -83.434548

Contact Information

BLUE RIDGE PARKWAY
199 Hemphill Knob Road
Asheville, NC 28803
828-348-3400, nps.gov/blri

CAESARS HEAD STATE PARK
8155 Geer Highway
Cleveland, SC 29635
864-836-6115
southcarolinaparks.com/caesarshead

CHIMNEY ROCK STATE PARK
PO Box 39
Chimney Rock, NC 28720
828-625-9611, chimneyrockpark.com

DOUTHAT STATE PARK
14239 Douthat State Park Road
Millboro, VA 24460
540-862-8100
dcr.virginia.gov/state-parks/douthat

DuPONT STATE FOREST
PO Box 300
Cedar Mountain, NC 28718
828-877-6527
dupontstaterecreationalforest.com

**EASTERN BAND OF THE
CHEROKEE NATION**
88 Council House Loop
Cherokee, NC 28719
828-497-7000, ebci.com

**GEORGE WASHINGTON AND
JEFFERSON NATIONAL FORESTS**
5162 Valleypointe Parkway
Roanoke, VA 24019
888-265-0019, fs.usda.gov/gwj

GORGES STATE PARK
976 Grassy Ridge Road
Sapphire, NC 28774
828-966-9099
ncparks.gov/gorges-state-park

**GREAT SMOKY MOUNTAINS
NATIONAL PARK**
107 Park Headquarters Road
Gatlinburg, TN 37738
865-436-1200, nps.gov/grsm

HANGING ROCK STATE PARK
1790 Hanging Rock Park Road
Danbury, NC 27016
336-593-8480
ncparks.gov/hanging-rock-state-park

**NANTAHALA AND PISGAH
NATIONAL FORESTS**
160 Zillicoa Street, Suite A
Asheville, NC 28801
828-257-4200, fs.usda.gov/nfsnc

NATURAL BRIDGE OF VIRGINIA
15 Appledore Lane
Natural Bridge, VA 24578
540-291-2121, naturalbridgeva.com

SHENANDOAH NATIONAL PARK
3655 US 211 E.
Luray, VA 22835
540-999-3500, nps.gov/shen

SOUTH MOUNTAINS STATE PARK
3001 S. Mountain Park Avenue
Connelly Springs, NC 28612
828-433-4772
ncparks.gov/south-mountains-state-park

STONE MOUNTAIN STATE PARK
3042 Frank Parkway
Roaring Gap, NC 28668
336-957-8185
ncparks.gov/stone-mountain
-state-park

THERE IS MORE MINISTRIES
7935 Parkway Road
Balsam Grove, NC 28708
828-884-6350, thereismoreministries.com

Index

About the Author

photo: Keri Anne Molloy

Johnny Molloy is a writer and adventurer, based in East Tennessee, who has lived in the shadow of the mountains for more than three decades. His outdoor passion started on a backpacking trip in Great Smoky Mountains National Park. That first foray unleashed a love of the outdoors that has led to his spending countless nights backpacking, canoe camping, and tent camping for the past 30 years. Friends enjoyed his outdoor adventure stories; one even suggested he write a book. He soon parlayed his love of the outdoors into an occupation. The results of his efforts are more than 75 books. His writings include hiking, camping, and paddling guidebooks; comprehensive guidebooks about a specific area; and true outdoor adventure books. Molloy has also written numerous articles for magazines, websites, and newspapers. He continues writing and traveling extensively throughout the United States, endeavoring in a variety of outdoor pursuits. His other interests include serving God as a Gideon, studying American history, and following University of Tennessee sports. For the latest on Johnny, please visit johnnymolloy.com.

DEAR CUSTOMERS AND FRIENDS,

SUPPORTING YOUR INTEREST IN OUTDOOR ADVENTURE, travel, and an active lifestyle is central to our operations, from the authors we choose to the locations we detail to the way we design our books. Menasha Ridge Press was incorporated in 1982 by a group of veteran outdoorsmen and professional outfitters. For many years now, we've specialized in creating books that benefit the outdoors enthusiast.

Almost immediately, Menasha Ridge Press earned a reputation for revolutionizing outdoors- and travel-guidebook publishing. For such activities as canoeing, kayaking, hiking, backpacking, and mountain biking, we established new standards of quality that transformed the whole genre, resulting in outdoor-recreation guides of great sophistication and solid content. Menasha Ridge Press continues to be outdoor publishing's greatest innovator.

The folks at Menasha Ridge Press are as at home on a whitewater river or mountain trail as they are editing a manuscript. The books we build for you are the best they can be, because we're responding to your needs. Plus, we use and depend on them ourselves.

We look forward to seeing you on the river or the trail. If you'd like to contact us directly, visit us at menasharidge.com. We thank you for your interest in our books and the natural world around us all.

SAFE TRAVELS,

Bob Sehlinger

BOB SEHLINGER
PUBLISHER